100 CATS WHO CHANGED CIVILIZATION

Library of Congress Cataloging in Publication
Number: 2006937818

ISBN: 978-1-59474-163-0

Printed in China

Typeset in Century Book

Designed by Bryn Ashburn
Illustrations by Gina Triplett

Distributed in North America by Chronicle Books
680 Second Street
San Francisco, CA 94107

10 9 8 7 6 5 4 3 2

Quirk Books
215 Church Street
Philadelphia, PA 19106
www.quirkbooks.com

100 CATS WHO CHANGED CIVILIZATION

HISTORY'S MOST INFLUENTIAL FELINES

BY SAM STALL

QUIRK BOOKS

PHILADELPHIA

To Ted.
He might not have been
the greatest cat in the world,
but he was the greatest
in mine.

CONTENTS

INTRODUCTION

"Cats are a mysterious kind of folk. There is more passing in their minds than we are aware of."
—Sir Walter Scott

Cats have communed with mankind since before the dawn of civilization. Yet discovering the handful who helped shape our history was no easy task. The typical feline is blithely uninterested in the comings and goings of the human race. It's part—perhaps the most important part—of their character. The people around them can do as they like, so long as there is food in the food dish, clean litter in the litter box, and a sunny window ledge from which to watch the world go by.

Nevertheless, over the centuries certain individuals of the feline persuasion have seen fit to exert themselves on humanity's behalf. For the most part they do it in their own distinctive way, for their own inscrutable reasons. Blatant grandstanding, such as, say, rescuing a toddler from a burning tenement, just isn't their style. Those escapades are best left to dogs.

Instead of showing off, many of the cats profiled in the following pages earned their laurels in more subtle ways. These luminaries could be divided into four broad groups: muses, pioneers, antiheroes, and heroes.

The muses made their marks by willingly giving companionship, inspiration, or even a simple morale boost to needy geniuses. Cattarina (page 90), the feline associate of Edgar Allan Poe, served as a template for one of the greatest horror stories ever written. And it was a tomcat named Macek (page 17) who inspired scientist Nicola Tesla to begin his world-changing study of electricity.

Some of the "pioneers" earned spots in the history books without even knowing it. A Canadian cat named Snowball (page 14) was quite unaware that a few strands of her hair not only caught a killer, but revolutionized criminal forensics as well. Likewise, one can rest assured that a feline named F. D. C. Willard (page 22) never knew he coauthored a research paper on low-energy physics. Furthermore, a black cat called Colby (page 73) hasn't the slightest inkling that he was awarded an executive MBA.

Of course, not all cats who changed history did so for the better. Thankfully, this small rogue's gallery of antiheroes is likewise ignorant of its misdeeds. A lighthouse keeper's pet named Tibbles (page 12) never knew that he was the only creature to single-handedly wipe out an entire species. And a kitten named Ahmedabad (page 61) was spared all knowledge of the serious diplomatic row he triggered between Pakistan and the United States.

Finally, this book would be remiss were it not to enumerate the sagas of classic hero cats—felines who during a crisis displayed such human-centric characteristics as bravery, resourcefulness, and resolve. To this elite group belongs Mourka (page 160), who assisted Russian forces during the bloody battle for Stalingrad; Trixy (page 169), who stood by her human associate during his imprisonment in the infamous Tower of London; and Tommy (page 162), who used a phone to call the police when his wheelchair-bound owner was incapacitated.

All these felines, plus the dozens of others enshrined in these pages, changed history in small—and sometimes not-so-small—ways. Their indifference, indeed their *obliviousness* to their achievements, could serve as an example for vain humans, many of whom make a much bigger fuss over much more modest accomplishments.

SCIENCE AND NATURE

TIBBLES

THE CAT WHO WIPED OUT
AN ENTIRE SPECIES

Felines are famous for their skill at eradicating mice, rats, and birds. But no cat in the history of civilization can match the unbridled bloodlust displayed by a humble lighthouse keeper's pet named Tibbles. He's become famous—or rather, infamous—in the annals of science as the only animal to have wiped out an entire species by itself.

The unlucky species in question was the Stephens Island wren. By all accounts, it was as unusual as it was harmless. Because there were originally no mice in the corner of the world where it evolved, the wren adapted to fill that ecological niche. It lost the ability to fly, shrank to roughly the size of a rodent, and spent its days running at top speed through the underbrush. But though it couldn't fly, the wren retained the ability to sing.

At one time this fragile, musical, mouselike bird called all of New Zealand home. But when South Pacific islanders arrived, they brought stowaway rats on their ships—rats that quickly invaded the local ecosystem. The wrens, completely helpless against the sudden onslaught of such a powerful and ruthless predator, were quickly exterminated. Their last rat-free redoubt was Stephens Island, a

roughly one-square-mile spit of rock off New Zealand's northern coast.

That's how matters stood until 1894, when a lighthouse was established there. Its keeper, David Lyall, brought along his cat, Tibbles, for company. One can only imagine the feline's delight at finding the island overrun with bite-sized, flightless birds. Not surprisingly, Tibbles got straight to work, attacking the little creatures wherever he found them.

Tibbles alerted his owner to his new hobby by hauling more than a dozen of his victims back to the lighthouse, all of them dead or nearly so. Lyall kept several, which because of their strangeness found their way into the hands of ornithologists. In 1895 the little animal was unveiled to the scientific world and given the Latin name *Xenicus lyalli*. Then, almost in the same breath, it was declared extinct.

The ecological destruction inaugurated by a pack of rats was, ironically, completed by a lone cat. It never occurred to the lighthouse keeper, or anyone else, that given the unique (and uniquely fragile) nature of the Stephens Island fauna, it might have been a good idea to make Tibbles an *indoor* cat.

SNOWBALL

THE CAT WHO CAUGHT A KILLER

Douglas Beamish thought he got away with murder. And he might have, if it weren't for the case-making evidence furnished by his cat.

It happened in 1994, when Canadian authorities on Prince Edward Island found Shirley Duguay buried in a shallow grave. Royal Canadian Mounted Police were called in to investigate. They paid particular attention to a blood-soaked leather jacket in a plastic bag that had been buried along with the body. Unfortunately, the blood was all Duguay's, and therefore useless for DNA comparisons. But forensics experts discovered something else: twenty-seven strands of white hair that, upon closer examination, were determined to come from a cat. The Mounties recalled that Beamish, Duguay's estranged common-law husband, lived not too far from the grave site with his parents—and that they owned a white feline named Snowball.

The Mounties obtained a blood sample from Snowball, hoping to compare it to the DNA in the hairs. The problem, they soon discovered, was that no one had ever done such a thing before. After a series of calls, the authorities located perhaps the only people on the planet who could help—a team of researchers at the National Cancer Institute's Laboratory of Genomic Diversity in Frederick, Maryland, which was developing a map of the feline genome.

The academics had never before participated in a *CSI*-style criminal investigation, and it took some convincing to get them on board. Once they signed on, however, they were able to quickly isolate the genetic code in the jacket hairs and match it to the blood sample from Snowball. Using this evidence, and the expert testimony of the scientists who developed the technology, Beamish was convicted of murder and sent to prison. The case set a precedent for the use of cat DNA to place criminals at the scenes of crimes. Afterward, the U.S. Department of Justice awarded a $265,000 grant to create a National Feline Genetic Database. It developed the technology necessary to help forensics labs around the world trace cat hairs found at crime scenes to specific pets. Thanks to Snowball, criminals (about a third of whom own felines) can now be busted by their own furry friends.

MACEK

THE CAT WHO GLOWED
IN THE DARK

Physicist, electrical engineer, and inventor Nikola Tesla is considered one of the most prolific and enigmatic geniuses of all time. In addition to pioneering the systems that made home electricity practical, he was instrumental in developing radio. His more futuristic pursuits included building machines to communicate with extraterrestrials, creating remote-controlled vehicles, and even attempting to refute Einstein's work on a unified field theory.

This was pretty heady stuff for a man born in 1856. He was definitely ahead of his time. When Tesla, who became a U.S. citizen, died in a New York City hotel room in 1943 at the age of eighty-six, the FBI swooped down on his residence, rounded up his papers, and sealed them in a secret file. In his later years the great scientist was rumored to be tinkering with a "death ray." The powers that be couldn't afford not to believe it.

From his youth, Tesla was fascinated by the unknown—a fascination inspired by his cat. He grew up in an isolated farmhouse in what is now Croatia. As a child, his beloved companion was a large feline named Macek (Serbian for "male cat"). Tesla, who described his four-legged friend as "the

finest of all cats in the world," went everywhere
with him.

As a boy of three, Tesla displayed no particular
interest in science. But during one particularly
cold and dry winter day, a huge charge of static
electricity built up in the atmosphere. People who
walked in the snow left glowing footprints, and
snowballs exploded like fireworks when they were
thrown against walls or trees.

But that was nothing compared to what happened to Macek. "In the dusk of the evening, as I

stroked Macek's back, I saw a miracle that made me speechless with amazement," Tesla wrote in later years. "Macek's back was a sheet of light and my hand produced a shower of sparks loud enough to be heard all over the house." Even more amazing, when the cat walked through darkened rooms, he faintly glowed.

The sight fired the boy's imagination, and sent him on a lifelong quest to understand electricity. Some say that Tesla, through his work, helped make the twentieth century possible. If so, then the world also owes a debt to Macek, who inspired him.

BLACKBERRY
THE QUEEN OF THE MUNCHKINS

Some cat breeds sport long hair, some short, some almost none. Some are lithe and athletic, others stocky and sedentary. All these differences have been readily accepted by cat fanciers, save one. In the early 1990s, the breeding community was set afire by a new kind of feline with very short legs. It was called the munchkin, and it is, without doubt, the world's most controversial cat.

The saga began in 1983 in Rayville, Louisiana. A woman named Sandra Hochenedel found two cats trying to escape a bulldog by hiding under a pick-up truck. Both were pregnant, and both had unusually short legs that made them look like a cross between a ferret and a dachshund. Hochenedel named the gray one Blueberry and gave it away. She named the black one Blackberry and kept it.

Blackberry promptly produced a litter of kittens, including a short-legged male. Hochenedel named him Toulouse and gave him to a friend, Kay LaFrance of Monroe, Louisiana. There Toulouse contributed enthusiastically to the local gene pool. Soon there were many short-legged cats and kittens slinking around the property. The two women, curious about the health of the little creatures, had them examined by Dr. Solveig Pflueger, chief of the genetics committee for The International Cat Association (TICA). She offered the opinion that the munchkins were physically sound. Interestingly, this sort of mutation seems to arise regularly. During the twentieth century, similar short-legged cats were reported everywhere from Russia to Germany to Great Britain.

Not everyone saw it that way, however. For years munchkin breeders were given the cold shoulder by cat shows and breed organizations, most of which saw them as unhealthy genetic aberrations. Words such as *freak* and *abomination* were used liberally. Munchkin owners were sometimes ejected from competitions. When TICA finally recognized Blackberry's progeny as a new breed in 1995, one veteran cat show judge resigned in protest, describing the cats as "an affront to any breeder with ethics."

In spite—or perhaps because—of the controversy, the munchkin has gained worldwide fame. The demand for munchkin kittens keeps rising, with some costing thousands of dollars. All because of poor Blackberry. Ever an outdoor cat, she one day simply vanished from Hochenedel's property—unaware or unconcerned that she was the founder of a dynasty.

F. D. C. WILLARD

THE CAT WHO TAUGHT US PHYSICS

Few humans can match the academic achievements ascribed to a certain Siamese named Felis Domesticus Chester (F. D. C.) Willard. He proved his mental mettle by coauthoring—with his human companion, Michigan State University professor J. H. Hetherington—two research papers on low-energy physics.

Willard earned his unique place in scientific history thanks to a typing issue. When Hetherington asked an associate to proof an article before submission, he was told that because he was the sole author, the piece couldn't be published until the editorial *we*—used throughout—was changed to *I*. Nowadays this could be accomplished using the "find and replace all" function on one's computer. But this was 1975, and Hetherington would have to spend days retyping.

Instead, he found a collaborator. He gave F. D. C. Willard second billing on the title page of his article, which was duly published in *Physical Review Letters*. The piece was so warmly received that in 1980 Hetherington presented a second scholarly work under his cat's name alone. The subterfuge was finally exposed when a visitor to Hetherington's office, upon learning the professor was out, asked to see Willard instead.

SIR ISAAC NEWTON'S CAT
THE INSPIRATION FOR THE CAT DOOR

Physicist Sir Isaac Newton was one of history's greatest mathematicians and theorists. During his lifetime he made numerous contributions to science, including developing the laws of celestial mechanics, codeveloping calculus, and conducting groundbreaking work on everything from the nature of light spectra to measurements of the speed of sound. But few realize that Newton was also a pet lover—or that sometimes his numerous animal friends could drive him to distraction. For instance, he once suffered an emotional breakdown when a favorite dog knocked over a candle on his desk, burning some of his important research notes.

His dealings with an annoying cat yielded happier results. The world's felines (and canines, for that matter) owe an everlasting debt of gratitude to this overbearing pet, whose name is lost to history. According to legend, it constantly interrupted Newton with its demands to be let in and out of the house. Frustrated, the scientist quickly designed and implemented a solution—the pet door. Today, every feline blessed with the ability to enter and leave a room without troubling his or her human friends has Newton (and his restless charge) to thank.

TEE CEE
THE CAT WHO PREDICTED SEIZURES

Were it not for their quirky, independent person-
alities, cats might be naturals for all sorts of jobs
usually done by service dogs. Keenly observant
and alert to the slightest changes in their
surroundings, felines could make wonderful
guardians. So far, however, they've firmly rejected
any such callings.

All save for one.

The cat in question is named Tee Cee, and he has
earned international fame for his uncanny ability
to predict epileptic seizures—a skill he's used to
ease the suffering of his grateful owner.
Ironically, the English feline had endured quite a
bit at the hands of a human, who stuffed Tee Cee
and his littermates in a box and tossed it in a
river. He was rescued and taken to an adoption
center, where he became the pet of Michael
Edmonds, a Sheffield man who suffers from an
extremely dangerous and unpredictable form of
epilepsy. The disorder causes sudden, violent
seizures that strike without warning. The problem
is so serious that Edmonds can't leave home
unescorted, for fear of having an attack at some
unexpected time or place.

Edmonds's new cat provided almost providential

help. Tee Cee took a great deal of interest in his new owner—particularly, it seemed, when he was about to seize. This was remarkable, because Edmonds displays no symptoms prior to attacks. Or at least, none detectable by humans. "We noticed that Tee Cee began staring at my stepfather prior to a seizure and then ran to my mother to let her know all is not well, acting as an early warning system," Edmonds's stepdaughter, Samantha Laidler, told the BBC. "Once assistance arrives, Tee Cee doesn't leave Michael's side until he regains consciousness, and his warnings have proved invaluable to the family."

The behavior was so unexpected that it took a while for family members to make the connection between Tee Cee's staring sessions and Edmonds's epileptic fits. But once the link was established, the fame of the former stray spread far and wide. In 2006 he was nominated for a prestigious Rescue Cat of the Year Award—quite an accomplishment for a feline who was once, literally, thrown away as garbage.

CC

THE CAT WHO WAS A CLONE

This cleverly named creature won fame for being both the most unique and un-unique of cats. Born in late 2001 in a blaze of publicity, CC (short for Copy Cat) was the world's first cloned feline.

The mostly gray calico was the crowning achievement of a research program originally established to clone dogs. In 1997, millionaire entrepreneur John Sperling bankrolled a roughly $4 million effort to develop a replacement for his beloved mutt, Missy. After years of work on what came to be known as the Missyplicity Project, scientists at Texas A&M University learned one key fact about cloning canines: It's hard. Cats, however, are relatively easier.

Emphasis on *relatively*. The group endured eighty-seven failures before producing CC. In 2000, Sperling and others founded a company to offer the process to grieving pet owners who pined for duplicates of their dearly departed friends—and could pay somewhere in the middle five figures to get them.

The birth of CC seemed to validate the business model of the company that created her. Bereaved but well-heeled former cat owners could turn to an organization whose name, Genetic Savings & Clone, sounded like something from an old *Outer*

Limits episode. The company ramped up its program to something approaching mass production. Clients with an eye toward the future could PetBank some of their cat's premortem DNA for future use in the Nine Lives Extravaganza cloning program. Then, when the original pet passed away, scientists at the company's state-of-the-art Madison, Wisconsin, laboratory could use that genetic information to create an embryo to be carried by a surrogate cat mom.

Is it possible to put a price tag on such a miracle? Actually, yes. Cat owners can make a deposit in the PetBank for around $1,000, and get a copy of their kitty for roughly $32,000.

Unfortunately for the company's backers, not enough people wanted carbon copies of their deceased kitties. Genetic Savings & Clone went out of business in late 2006. Interestingly, even though the firm trafficked in clones, it couldn't guarantee that the cats it created would be exact copies of the originals. Nature, it seems, hates to repeat itself. Though the company's clones carried the same genetic code as the original animals, environmental factors sometimes introduced slight—or not-so-slight—variations. For instance, while CC is an exact genetic duplicate of her DNA donor (a calico tabby named Rainbow), her fur is a different color.

ACOUSTIC KITTY

THE CAT THE CIA TURNED INTO A BUG

The mysterious world of espionage reached its pinnacle during the darkest days of the Cold War. As the Soviet Union and the West struggled for worldwide military and economic supremacy, no intelligence-gathering scheme seemed too wild or harebrained if it offered a chance, however small, of gaining vital information.

Yet, even in the context of those desperate times, the CIA's plan to turn a stray cat into an electronic intelligence gathering platform still sounds rather, well, *nuts*.

The project was revealed to the public in 2001, when it was mentioned in a passel of heavily censored documents declassified by the CIA's Science and Technology Directorate. According to experts, the scheme, hatched during the 1960s, was to wire felines with listening equipment so they could eavesdrop on conversations. The prototype, called Acoustic Kitty, was surgically implanted with microphones, batteries, and a radio receiver, along with an antenna running up its tail. The $16 million project came to an abrupt end, however, during field trials. The bionic cat was released near a park and was promptly run over by a taxi.

It was a merciful finale for the poor creature.

Perhaps God—or Mother Nature, or simply fate—realized that a bunch of idiots were tampering with biology's most elegant design and decided to stage an intervention.

ALL BALL

THE CAT WHO PLAYED
WITH A GORILLA

Scientists once believed that the ability to make and use tools was a skill reserved only for humans. Now they've realized that creatures from chimps to certain kinds of birds can master this trick. So are there *any* behaviors that set us apart from the "lower" animals? Perhaps our inclination to keep other species as pets makes us unique.

Or perhaps not.

If the behavior of Koko the gorilla is any guide, other creatures crave this sort of companionship, too. The Woodside, California, resident, born in 1976, is world famous for her "speaking" ability. The scientists who care for her assert that she's learned more than 1,000 American Sign Language symbols and uses them to communicate everything from her physical needs to her moods.

In 1984, Koko reportedly told her keepers that she'd like to have a pet cat for her birthday present. Shortly thereafter, a litter of abandoned kittens was brought in for her to inspect. After carefully examining each one, she chose a tailless gray male who she named All Ball. Though Koko was of course far larger and much stronger than her fragile new charge, she treated him with great gentleness.

All Ball was cuddled, kissed, and allowed to ride around on Koko's back like a baby gorilla.

Sadly, All Ball escaped from the compound in December 1984 and was killed by a car. Koko was inconsolable. She cried for days and tried to express her loss to her keepers through sign language. When someone asked what happened to her pet, Koko responded by signing "Sleep cat." And when she was shown a picture of a kitten that looked like All Ball, she signed, "Cry, sad, frown."

Can a gorilla really communicate using language? Maybe, or maybe not. Some scientists wonder if Koko truly comprehends what she's doing, or if, perhaps, the words she uses are merely wishful thinking on the part of the handlers who interpret for her. But what's harder to dispute is the depth of the gorilla's reaction to her small friend's death. Koko may or may not be able to sign the word for grief, but she certainly seems to feel it.

SCHRÖDINGER'S CAT

THE MOST ENIGMATIC CAT IN OUR UNIVERSE. OR ANY UNIVERSE, FOR THAT MATTER

For more than a century, physicists have struggled to understand quantum mechanics—the rules governing the behavior of subatomic particles. This is important because the knowledge is essential for everything from nuclear power to computer science to genetic engineering. But it's also maddening, because these incredibly small objects don't behave in ways the average person would consider normal. Or even rational.

One of the most bedeviling problems is that while in the "big" universe one can chart the positions of planets and stars based on mathematical formulas, the subatomic world's behavior can't be easily predicted. For instance, it is physically impossible to determine both the momentum and precise position of an electron orbiting an atomic nucleus. What this means, in layman's terms, is that our entire known world is constructed of things that can't ever be known.

Great minds have expended enormous quantities of chalk and covered numberless chalkboards trying to reconcile the operation of the tiny quantum universe with our "real" world. In 1934, physicist

Erwin Schrödinger tried to illustrate those complexities by using, of all things, an imaginary cat.

Schrödinger designed a thought experiment in which an atomic nucleus was used in a game of automated Russian roulette with a theoretical feline. Writing in the German magazine *Natural Sciences*, he ruminated about what might happen if a cat were placed in a sealed box with a canister of poison gas that was connected in some way to a radioactive atomic nucleus. The nucleus has an exactly 50 percent chance of decaying in one hour. If it does, its radiation will open the gas canister, killing the cat. If it doesn't decay, the canister won't open and the cat will survive.

Here's where things get strange. According to our understanding of quantum mechanics, subatomic particles such as the nucleus could exist in many states at once, until some sort of outside stimulus forced them into one course of action. In the world of quantum physics, *the mere act of observation* can accomplish this. In other words, someone looking at it could cause the nucleus to stop fluxing between multiple states and, in essence, pick a side. Thus, an observer who opened the box after an hour would find either a dead cat or a live cat.

But what goes on inside the container *before* the human looks and forces the nucleus down one road or the other? According to some interpretations of quantum theory, inside this *Twilight Zone* of a box, both things happen at once. The nucleus is both decayed and undecayed, and the cat is both alive and dead. Furthermore, some physicists assert that when the box is finally opened and the results observed, *both* alternatives continue. Time and space split, and two entire universes shear off from each other—one in which the cat lives, the other in which it dies.

Not surprisingly, Schrödinger's enigmatic cat has become a feline celebrity among the learned. Sly references show up regularly in science fiction movies and television series such as *Dr. Who* and *Futurama*, and writers from Ursula K. Le Guin to Robert A. Heinlein have coopted the feline in their books.

That's a lot of press for an animal that isn't real. However, fans can take comfort in the fact that while Schrödinger's cat doesn't exist in *this* corner of the space-time continuum, it may in some other bit of the quantum-ruled Multiverse.

OTHER FELINES OF DISTINCTION

THE FIRST KNOWN DOMESTIC CAT—Discovered by French archaeologists in a 9,500-year-old grave on the island of Cyprus. Near its final resting place sits the grave of (presumably) its human master.

THE DOCTOR'S DEVILS—The nickname of matching black cats owned by eighteenth-century London quack Gustavus Katterfelto, who conned the gullible by displaying "scientific wonders" such as rudimentary electricity tricks. Katterfelto used the static that built up in the cats' fur to, literally, put the spark in his presentations.

SIZI—The prized pet of physician and theologian Dr. Albert Schweitzer. If Sizi fell asleep on Schweitzer's left arm, he refused to use that limb until his feline friend moved of her own accord.

TAMA—Created in 2000 by Japan's Omron corporation, Tama was the first mass-produced robotic feline. Pressure sensors enabled her to detect and react to petting.

THE HYPOALLERGENIC CAT—Recently produced by the San Diego-based company Allerca, these felines are genetically engineered to suppress a protein secretion that causes allergies.

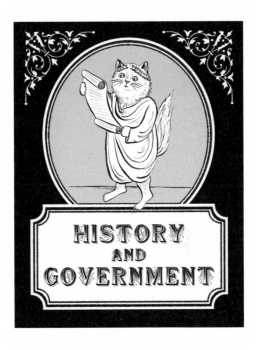

HISTORY
AND
GOVERNMENT

NADJEM

THE FIRST CAT WITH A NAME

It is widely believed that domestic cats evolved from the African wildcat, a tabby-like creature called *Felis silvestris libyca*, along the banks of the Nile River. The first farmers, desperate to defend their hard-won stores of grain from rats and mice, were doubtless overjoyed when these small, lithe predators took up residence near their granaries, looking for easy kills. They were so happy, in fact, that they perhaps went out of their way to attract them and to see to their comfort.

It wasn't long before those wild hunters became thoroughly domesticated, insinuating themselves not just into Egyptian homes, but into Egyptian culture as well. The cat goddess Bast became a popular cult figure, as did another, more sinister feline deity called Sekhmet. Felines in general were considered divine messengers, and killing one was taboo. Those who did so, even by accident, were often lynched on the spot by angry mobs. Pampered housecats wore earrings, nose rings, and expensive collars, and upon death they were often mummified and given lavish burials. Hundreds of thousands of cat mummies have been discovered all over Egypt.

And yet, though their pictures adorned everything from palace walls to scrolls to jewelry, very little was written or said about individual cats. Most, it is believed, didn't even have names. They were all referred to simply as *mau*, which literally means "he who mews."

That's what makes one particular cat, who lived and died during the reign of Pharaoh Thutmose III (1479–1425 BC), so unique. The feline in question was called Nadjem (meaning "dear one" or, perhaps, "star"). Nadjem was mentioned on the wall of the tomb of a low-level functionary named Puimre, who was interred outside the ancient city of Thebes.

There's little else to say about Nadjem, other than that Puimre must have loved him (or her) a great deal. Too bad he can never know the enormity of the boon he bestowed upon his pet. By choosing to preserve his cat's moniker for posterity, he made him (or her) the first feline in recorded history who we can call by name.

MUEZZA

THE CAT WHO WAS MOHAMMED'S FAVORITE PET

Christianity has always viewed the cat with suspicion. Over the centuries the poor creature has been accused of every conceivable crime, from stealing the breath of newborns to serving as Satan's minion. Islam, however, takes the opposite view. The cat is so highly esteemed that it is even allowed in mosques.

Felines owe this exalted status to Muezza, the adored pet of the Prophet Mohammed. One day, as his faithful pet slept on one of the sleeves of his robe, Mohammed was called away to prayer. Rather than disturb the cat, he cut off the sleeve. When he returned, Muezza bowed to his master and received three strokes down her back in return. This blessing assured her a spot in the afterlife.

According to other tales, Mohammed would give sermons in his home with Muezza nestled in his lap. The stories are unclear as to what type of cat she was. However, this hasn't stopped feline fanciers around the world from stating that she was everything from a tabby to an Angora to an Abyssinian.

DICK WHITTINGTON'S CAT

THE CAT WHO LAUNCHED
A POLITICAL CAREER

Situated atop London's Highgate Hill stands a statue of a feline known simply as Dick Whittington's cat. According to legend, he belonged to a man named Richard Whittington, who lived from 1350 to 1423 and served as mayor of London four times. Yet it is doubtful he would be remembered at all were it not for the stories about his wonderful pet—a pet who, in real life, he probably never possessed.

A great deal is known about the real Dick Whittington. He was the younger son of Sir William Whittington, Lord of the Manor of Pauntley in Gloucestershire. He made a fortune selling fine cloth and was on good terms with both King Richard II and his successor, King Henry IV. He married a woman named Alice Fitzwarren and, of course, served as London's mayor. After his death, he willed his vast fortune to charity.

And then something strange happened—something that would transform the real Whittington into the hero of a childhood fable. The people of London, anxious to know more about their benefactor, invented a biography that centered around, of all things, a cat. The centuries-old account casts Whittington as a poor country lad who came to the big city to make a name for himself. He worked for a merchant named Fitzwarren and fell in love with Alice, his daughter. His sole possession was a cat, whom he gave to a sea captain to sell during his voyage.

Sometime afterward, Whittington decided to return to his hometown of Gloucestershire. But as he trudged past Highgate Hill he heard the city's bells tolling. They seemed to say, "Turn again, Whittington, three times Lord Mayor of London." So he went back to Fitzwarren's house, where he learned that the captain he'd given his cat to had returned with incredible news. A foreign potentate whose palace was overrun by rats had bought the cat, paying with a huge pile of gold. Dick instantly became wealthy, married Alice, and eventually became Lord Mayor of London three times as predicted, plus an additional term.

The tale became (and remains) a popular children's story retold regularly in books, plays, and pantomimes. One doubts that the real Whittington would mind. The cat with whom he shares the limelight has won him lasting fame.

THE CATERER
THE CAT WHO USED PIGEONS
TO HELP A JAILBIRD

Throughout most of human history, politics was a winner-take-all proposition in which losers forfeited their fortunes and lives. Such was almost the case for Sir Henry Wyatt, who was born in Yorkshire, England, in 1460. During the two-year reign of King Richard III, he supported the claims of Henry Tudor, Earl of Richmond, to the throne. The king had Wyatt imprisoned in the Tower of London, where he was kept in freezing conditions, tortured, and fed a starvation diet.

But one day a feline walked through the grate covering the cell's window and made the acquaintance of the room's emaciated inmate. Wyatt, overjoyed to have company, petted and praised the cat. The two became fast friends, and the stray promptly set about saving its human companion's life by killing pigeons and fetching them to Wyatt's cell.

The famished prisoner gladly accepted them, and he convinced one of his jailers to dress and cook the birds. Soon the feline was referred to as Wyatt's *acater* (caterer). Thus fortified, Wyatt held out against all adversity until, finally, Richard III was ousted from the throne by Henry Tudor, who was crowned Henry VII. Needless to

say, the former prisoner's prospects rapidly improved. He was freed from the Tower, given wealth and title, and lived to the ripe old age of eighty.

Through it all he never forgot the kindness of the Tower cat, whose fate is unrecorded. One hopes that Wyatt found a way to help his benefactor, as he did almost every other cat he encountered. "Sir Henry in his prosperity would ever make much of a cat, and perhaps you will never find a picture of him anywhere, but with a cat beside him," said one historical account.

Today, the Church of St Mary the Virgin and All Saints in Maidstone features a stone memorial to Wyatt, "who was imprisoned and tortured in the Tower, in the reign of King Richard the third, kept in the dungeon, where fed and preserved by a cat." The monument is a touchstone of sorts for the extended Wyatt family, which thrives in both the United States and Canada—and would be all but extinct were it not for one resourceful feline.

MANEKI NEKO

THE FORLORN TEMPLE CAT
WHO BECAME JAPAN'S SYMBOL
OF GOOD FORTUNE

A visitor to almost any Japanese shop, restaurant, or bar will likely find, crouched near the entrance, a small porcelain statue of a cat. The cartoon-like creature may sport a slight smile and hold a gold coin cupped in one paw. The other paw (either the right or left) will be raised in a beckoning gesture. This is the famous Maneki Neko, or beckoning cat, a charm that supposedly attracts wealth and good fortune to anyone who displays it. But this creature may not be entirely mythological. According to Japanese legend, it is based on a real tortoiseshell tabby—a tabby whose timely invitation to a passing nobleman elevated a humble Buddhist shrine to wealth and fame.

Several different stories purport to tell what happened, but the following is the most commonly recounted: Sometime during Japan's Edo period (1603–1867), a nobleman rode past a rundown temple outside Tokyo. While passing, he happened to notice the temple master's cat, which seemed to beckon to him. Intrigued and perhaps slightly unnerved, he dismounted and approached. At that moment a lightning bolt struck the spot on the road he'd just left.

The noble, who believed the humble feline kept him from destruction, endowed his temple home with lands and money. Years later, when the cat who saved his life died, he had the first Maneki Neko figurine created in his honor. According to some versions of the tale, the place in question was the famous Gotoku-ji shrine near Tokyo. Whether this story is true is anyone's guess. However, the popularity of cat statues among the Japanese is indisputable. They have been produced by the millions, in versions ranging from

piggy banks to dashboard ornaments—all of them designed to attract money and luck to their owners, just as the original feline did.

The wings of pop culture have spread the talisman's influence around the world—sometimes in unexpected ways. One of the most famous Pokémon characters, Meowth, is an anime incarnation of Maneki Neko. And the ubiquitous Hello Kitty bears more than a passing resemblance to the famous feline. Even her name is considered by some to be a loose translation of that of the beckoning cat.

RUTTERKIN

THE CAT WHO WAS ACCUSED
OF MURDER

During the Middle Ages, European cats received some of the worst press in the history of the species. They were accused of being agents of evil and of serving as familiars for witches. Popes occasionally railed against them, and public disapproval of felines could grow so heated that they would be exterminated from entire towns.

One example of this overreaction took place in Lincoln, England, in 1618. Joan Flower and her daughters, Margaret and Philippa Flower, were accused by the local magistrates of using the dark arts to take revenge on their employers, the Earl and Countess of Rutland. History doesn't record the reasons for their ire. However, it describes their alleged methods in forensic detail. According to testimony from the women (extracted, as was usual at that time, under torture and intense interrogation), Joan Flower possessed a spirit familiar called Rutterkin, which manifested itself in the form of a sinister-looking black cat. The feline was their weapon of choice when casting spells. One favorite tactic was to steal gloves from members of the Earl's family, boil them, prick them full of holes, and then rub them along Rutterkin's back. According to court proceedings, this odd-sounding bewitchment accomplished the death of the Earl of Rutland's son, Lord Ross.

And what did the supposedly demonic cat get in exchange? In addition to the women's immortal souls, he also was allowed to feed on Joan Flower's blood.

The death of Lord Ross, plus various odd illnesses suffered by other close relations, finally drove the Earl of Rutland's family to believe that the Flowers were hatching some sort of plot against them. The women, after enduring all the usual inducements available to the medieval legal system, signed confessions. Joan died in custody, but her daughters were burned at the stake.

What became of Rutterkin? One hopes he had the good sense to simply slink away. His kind were maligned throughout Christendom, making it impossible for the hapless feline to get a fair hearing. Even today, in our supposedly enlightened era, his descendants are slandered in everything from Halloween cards to cheap, straight-to-video horror flicks. In a very real sense, today's black cats have one paw in the Dark Ages.

SINH

THE LEGENDARY CAT WHO
WAS THE FIRST BIRMAN

Few cat breeds have histories as colorful—or as steeped in violence—as the Birman. This elegant, distinctive-looking longhaired cat owes its existence to two redoubtable felines, one of them legendary, the other quite real.

The first, called Sinh, was supposedly one of a hundred snow-white, yellow-eyed cats inhabiting the Temple of Lao-Tsun in Burma. There the golden, blue-eyed, female goddess, who oversaw the transmutation of souls from one plane of existence to the next, was worshipped by the Khmer people of Southeast Asia. Sinh was a particular favorite of the shrine's chief monk, Mun-Ha.

One night raiders attacked the temple, mortally wounding Mun-Ha. As the monk lay dying, Sinh planted his feet on his master's chest and faced the golden statue of the goddess. Suddenly his white body turned to gold and his yellow eyes to sapphire blue. His legs turned brown like the earth, but his feet, where they touched the priest's body, became snow white as a symbol of purity. Not long afterward, all the other temple cats were similarly transformed.

Sinh, who had also taken up the soul of Mun-Ha, remained standing in front of the statue of

Lao-Tsun, his eyes locked on hers. He died after seven days, delivering the spirit of his master to heaven. Afterward, it was said that whenever a Birman temple cat expired, the soul of a dead priest accompanied it to paradise.

Ironically, a tragedy not unlike the one that inspired the story of Sinh was instrumental in bringing this exotic breed to the West. In the early years of the twentieth century, the ancient temple was once more attacked by raiders. This time, however, two outsiders, Englishmen Major Gordon Russell and his friend Auguste Pavie were on hand to assist the monks in repelling the assault. Years later, in 1919, the monks sent Pavie, who had relocated to Europe, a reward—a male and female Birman. The male died during the long sea voyage to his new home, but the female arrived safely, and she was pregnant. It is generally believed that this single feline and her kittens formed the root stock of the Western branch of the Birman family.

SIAM

AMERICA'S FIRST SIAMESE CAT

For centuries the world-famous Siamese cat could be found only in Siam (now Thailand). There they allegedly guarded Buddhist shrines and attended members of the royal family. It didn't hurt that they were also arrestingly beautiful. Then, as now, the typical Siamese sported a light-colored body with black feet, tail, and face, accented by glittering blue eyes.

These cats were destined to become one of the world's most popular breeds. But in the late 1800s, the creatures were largely unknown outside their home country. Their very first overseas ambassador went abroad in 1878, when David B. Sickels, a diplomat at the U.S. consulate in Bangkok, elected to send one to Lucy Hayes, wife of then-president Rutherford B. Hayes.

Considering everything the poor cat went through to reach America, one can understand why Siamese cats weren't exported much. The beleaguered feline traveled for two months, first going overland from Bangkok to Hong Kong, then by sea to San Francisco, then traversing the entire North American continent to Washington, D.C. She finally arrived at the White House, tucked inside a Wells Fargo crate, in early 1879.

The Hayes family was delighted, and named the

exotic-looking female Siam. She enjoyed the run of the executive mansion and made a habit of walking in on political functions, where her looks always caused a stir.

Sadly, her stateside tour didn't last long. In the fall of 1879, she fell ill. The White House staff plied her with every delicacy imaginable, and the president's personal physician, Dr. J. H. Baxter, was called in. He took Siam home with him so he could provide round-the-clock care, but to no avail. In October she finally expired.

The presidential family, the White House staff, and cat fanciers in general were greatly saddened, because Siam had made quite an impression during her brief stateside sojourn. Interestingly, the cat's remains may still reside somewhere in the bowels of the government. After Siam's death, the president's steward, Billy Crump, supposedly delivered her body to the Secretary of Agriculture, with instructions that it should be preserved. Whether this happened—and where the remains might be— is now an open question. Careful searches of the Department of Agriculture and of the Smithsonian Institution's vast holdings turned up neither hide nor hair of Siam.

TIGER

THE CAT WHO WAS KIDNAPPED
FROM THE WHITE HOUSE

Few felines have caused as much high-level con-
sternation as Tiger, one of the cats owned by the
thirtieth president of the United States, Calvin
Coolidge. Coolidge, who served from 1923 to 1929,
was arguably the most pet-friendly person ever to
sit in the Oval Office. During his two terms he
turned the White House into a veritable zoo. He and
his wife, Grace, brought in a gaggle of domesticated
birds ranging from canaries to a goose named
Enoch, a donkey called Ebenezer, a semiwild bob-
cat named Smokey, and a vast collection of canines
that included everything from collies to a Shetland
sheepdog to a bulldog. Foreign dignitaries,
apprised of the Coolidges' tastes, gave the couple
lion cubs, a bear, even a pygmy hippopotamus.

This immense cast of characters also included
two cats, Tiger and Blacky. Of the two, Tiger
seemed to grab the most headlines. The president
made a habit of walking around with the tabby
tomcat draped around his neck. During state functions, it was almost expected that at some point
the cat would saunter in, observe the proceedings,
and then wander back out.

Tiger's penchant for wandering eventually got
him into trouble. Back in Coolidge's day no one

thought of confining cats indoors—not even one belonging to the president of the United States. If the spirit moved him, Tiger was free to walk right through the iron fence surrounding 1600 Pennsylvania Avenue and explore Washington, D.C. The spirit, it appears, moved him quite often. Once, when he failed to return, the worried president took the desperate step of mentioning his absence during a radio address, asking anyone who saw Tiger to please send him home. The plea worked. Not too long afterward, the wayward kitty was spotted near the Lincoln Memorial, about a mile away, and taken back to the White House.

After that, Tiger was equipped with a green collar and Blacky with a red one. Both carried the words "The White House" engraved on a metal plate. Unfortunately, Tiger soon disappeared again, this time for good. In hindsight, Grace Coolidge wondered if perhaps the collars had been a mistake. They were intended as identification. In reality, they turned poor Tiger into the mother of all souvenirs.

OSCAR

THE CAT WHO SANK THE BISMARCK—ALONG WITH SEVERAL OTHER VESSELS

In May 1941, at the height of World War II, the mighty German battleship *Bismarck* was given orders to sail into the North Atlantic and attack the vast naval convoys hauling vital supplies from Canada and the United States to Great Britain. The *Bismarck*, considered one of the most powerful warships afloat, was uniquely qualified for the task. The British Royal Navy, desperate to preserve its lifeline to the New World, confronted the mighty ship as soon as it put to sea. After a bloody three-day fight, the vessel was pounded into scrap metal and sunk. Only a handful of its crew of thousands survived.

The lucky ones included the ship's cat, Oscar, who was picked up by the destroyer HMS *Cossack*. The crew renamed the black feline with the white chest Unsinkable Sam and made him their mascot. But there was nothing lucky about Sam. Within five months the *Cossack* was torpedoed by a German submarine and sent to the bottom of the sea. Again, the survivors included the cat, who took up residence on the aircraft carrier HMS *Ark Royal*. But only three weeks later, the *Ark Royal* was also torpedoed and sunk. Perhaps it was a sort of vengeance: One of the aircraft carrier's torpedo bombers had been responsible for damage to the *Bismarck*'s rudder, allowing Oscar's original home to be caught and destroyed.

Eerily, the feline once more escaped Davy Jones's locker, to be picked up by the destroyer HMS *Legion*. The authorities, perhaps afraid to let any creature so patently unlucky aboard another Royal Navy vessel, "retired" Oscar/Sam to dry land. He finished his long life at an old sailors' home in Belfast, passing away in 1955. Happily, he took no ships with him.

JOCK

THE CAT WHO BECAME
A HISTORIC LANDMARK

Winston Churchill was one of history's great cat lovers. Throughout his life there was almost always one—or more than one—nearby. One of the most famous included a pet simply named Cat. Once, when Cat ran away after Churchill yelled at him, he had a sign placed in the window of his home that read, "Cat, come home, all is forgiven." The feline did indeed return and was rewarded with special treats to regain his favor.

During World War II, Churchill's most high-profile companion at No. 10 Downing Street was Nelson, a large black tomcat who followed him everywhere, even into important meetings. Churchill said his companion contributed to the war effort by serving as "a prime ministerial hot water bottle." But perhaps the most enduring of all of Churchill's feline associates was—and remains—a marmalade cat given to him for his eighty-eighth birthday. Since the cat was a present from his private secretary, Sir John Colville, he was called by Colville's nickname, Jock.

The new addition to the household immediately became a great favorite. Jock was allowed to perch on Churchill's knee during formal photos that were taken for the wedding of one of his grandsons. But their time together was brief. Jock was only two years old when Churchill died in 1965. He actually sat on the bed with his master as the great man breathed his last. He remained at the family residence, Chartwell, until his own passing in 1974. He lies buried in a pet cemetery on the grounds.

But that wasn't the end of the story. Churchill's will left Chartwell to the government, which turned the estate into a national monument. There was, however, a stipulation: The property always had to have a marmalade cat named Jock in residence. Currently the job is handled by Jock III. Not surprisingly, having a cat roaming around a historic landmark can be somewhat of a pain. The home's conservators make sure the current Jock doesn't try his claws out on the furnishings or get at the bowl of goldfish that resides perpetually in Churchill's old study. Mostly he spends his days outdoors, catching the occasional mouse, sunning himself in the garden, and enjoying the largesse of a kindly master he will never know.

AHMEDABAD

THE CAT WHO SPARKED
AN INTERNATIONAL INCIDENT

At the beginning of the 1960s, famed U.S. diplomat John Kenneth Galbraith served for twenty-seven months as ambassador to India. During his tenure at that sensitive diplomatic station, he handled everything from the American response to the 1962 Sino-Indian war to disputes over his country's relationship with Pakistan. But those important developments pale in comparison to the embarrassing international incident touched off by a member of his own household—who wasn't even human. The greatest firestorm of Galbraith's tenure erupted over a misunderstanding involving his pet cat, Ahmedabad.

It began in 1962. During an official visit to the Indian state of Gujarat, Galbraith's two young sons were each given Siamese kittens. One received an utterly innocuous name and is forgotten by history. The other got what at the time must have *seemed* like an equally forgettable moniker—*Ahmedabad*, to commemorate the town in which it was born.

This probably would not have been a problem. Unfortunately, the Galbraith family shortened it to *Ahmed*. This, as they were soon to learn, is one of the many, many alternate names for the Muslim prophet Mohammed.

And that, as it turned out, was a *big* problem.

Shortly after the cat was innocently mentioned in a newspaper article, riots erupted across neighboring Pakistan, where the feline's name was taken as an insult to Islam. American facilities were stoned, U.S. personnel were attacked in the streets, and mullahs across the country called for Galbraith's head. "I do not think the Pakistanis were particularly sensitive," Galbraith wrote in his memoirs. "In the darker reaches of our Bible Belt, there would have been criticism of a Pakistan ambassador who, at a moment of friction between our two nations, had, however innocently, named his dog Jesus."

The crisis was finally ended when the diplomat explained, repeatedly and at great length, that the kitten was in no way, shape, or form named after a person—especially a religious prophet. Furthermore, to defuse any subsequent misunderstandings, it had been renamed Gujarat. Thus, with a meow rather than a roar, the incident faded away. "Amateurs will never understand how much can turn on the name of a kitten," an amused Galbraith wrote.

SMUDGE

THE CAT WHO JOINED A UNION

In Europe, it can be very hard to get ahead without belonging to a union. Such was the case for one beleaguered employee of the People's Palace, a museum and indoor conservatory located in Glasgow, Scotland. The worker in question was a former stray cat named Smudge. From 1979 until her retirement in 1990, she worked as the facility's mouser. Smudge became a celebrity, serving as the spokescat for various local groups and issues and lending her face to museum gift shop items ranging from ceramic statues to T-shirts. In 1987, when she vanished for three weeks, pleas from local dignitaries, including the Lord Provost of Glasgow, led to her discovery and return.

But Smudge's greatest claim to fame was her union card. First the museum staff put her up for membership in the National and Local Government Officers Association as a blue collar worker, but she was rejected. So instead she signed on with the General, Municipal and Boilermakers Trade Union, which happily included her in its ranks. She remained a staunch supporter of organized labor until her death in 2000.

HUMPHREY

ENGLAND'S MOST
CONTROVERSIAL CAT

English prime ministers have a long history of sharing No. 10 Downing Street with felines. There's more to it than mere affection, however. The sprawling government complex has something of a rodent problem, so the cats have always earned their keep.

A mouser named Humphrey was no exception. Found by a civil servant and named after a character on the popular British television show *Yes, Minister*, he started work in 1988 during the Margaret Thatcher administration, replacing a recently deceased tomcat named Wilberforce. For a government stipend of 100 pounds per year, Humphrey made life as hard, and as brief, as possible for the building's vermin. He served throughout the Thatcher administration and straight through that of her successor, John Major.

It was good that Humphrey had work to serve as a distraction from the numerous crises and controversies swirling around him. In 1994, the press accused him of killing a nest full of robin chicks that occupied a window box outside Major's office. The government, adopting peculiarly strong language, called the charges "libelous."

That was nothing compared with what happened in June 1995, when Humphrey suddenly vanished. The situation grew so grim that on September 25 the prime minister's office issued a memo lamenting the cat's assumed death. But shortly thereafter he turned up at the Royal Army Medical College, where he'd been adopted as a presumed stray and renamed PC (short for Patrol Car).

The most serious dustup took place when Major's conservative government was replaced by the administration of Tony Blair. Rumors quickly spread that the new prime minister's wife, Cherie, either didn't like Humphrey or was allergic to him. Finally, in November 1997 it was announced that the cat had been given to an anonymous elderly couple so that he could enjoy his "retirement." This in turn sparked stories that Humphrey had been euthanized—a tale that was squelched only when photos of him standing beside some current newspapers were taken at his new (and secret) residence.

The various controversies faded when Humphrey went to his final reward in March 2006. Happily, throughout his eventful tenure, the veteran mouser remained blissfully oblivious to it all.

BLACKIE

THE CAT WHO COULD
TALK—AND SUE

U.S. law books are filled with groundbreaking civil rights cases. One of the most entertaining concerns a talented black cat from South Carolina. According to his owners, Carl and Elaine Miles, they acquired him at a rooming house in the late 1970s, when a girl with a box of kittens asked if they wanted one. "I said no, I didn't want one," Carl recalled during court testimony. "As I was walking away from the box of kittens, a voice spoke to me and said, 'Take the black kitten.' I took the black kitten, knowing nothing else unusual or nothing else strange about the black kitten."

But things would soon get very unusual. A few months later Carl, inspired by what he called "the voice of God," became convinced that the kitten was attempting to talk to him. So he tried to help the process by developing what amounted to a speech therapy program for cats. First he taped the sounds Blackie made, then played them back to him. He also encouraged his pet to watch his master's lips as he spoke.

This effort paid off. The cat began, haltingly, to "talk" at six months. Shortly thereafter it could utter a grab bag of phrases clearly enough to become of interest to promoters. He talked (for a fee) on radio and television, and even made an appearance on the network program *That's Incredible*.

But then the feline thespian's fame subsided. By May 1981, the Mileses were reduced to exhibiting Blackie on the streets of Augusta, Georgia, where he would say things like "I want my mama" and "I love you" to passersby in exchange for handouts. Unfortunately, the local constabulary was less than charmed and insisted that the couple purchase a $50 business license. They complied, but then sued the city, stating that the law didn't specifically mention talking animals. This was enough to make the case interesting. But then the Mileses went on to assert that the fee *violated their right to free speech and association*. Not just theirs, but Blackie's too.

It was an interesting argument, to say the least, and one that might have eased the lives of noisy alley cats and chatty Siamese everywhere had the courts agreed with it. Unfortunately—though, perhaps, predictably—they didn't. The couple lost their case in district court, which stated that even though Augusta's business ordinance didn't specifically mention talking animals, what the Mileses did was certainly a business, and therefore in need of a license.

The case was then kicked upstairs to the U.S. Court of Appeals for the Eleventh District. It, too, agreed that the couple needed to pay Augusta the contested $50. And in a footnote, the three-judge panel saw fit to address the issue of Blackie's free speech rights, such as they were—or, in this case, weren't. "The Court will not hear a claim that Blackie's right to free speech has been infringed," they said. "First, although Blackie arguably possesses a very unusual ability, he cannot be considered a 'person' and is therefore not protected by the Bill of Rights. Second, even if Blackie had such a right, we see no need for appellants to assert his right *jus tertii* [as a third party]. Blackie can clearly speak for himself."

Thus ended the first attempt to gain free speech rights for cats. Not with a whimper, or even a meow, but with a quip.

CAT MANDU

THE FELINE WHO WAS
A TRUE PARTY ANIMAL

Few jobs offer as many chances for personal embarrassment and career-destroying scandals as that of political party boss. That's what makes the spotless career of one Cat Mandu of Great Britain so exemplary. For several years he helped lead a high-profile—albeit not very powerful—political organization. If there was trouble, he always landed on his feet. And if there was controversy, he knew how to keep his mouth shut.

Actually, he had little choice on that count. Because he couldn't talk. Because he was a cat. Specifically, a large ginger tomcat owned by Alan Hope, who was also known as Howling Laud Hope.

What sort of organization would grant leadership to a feline? None other than the Official Monster Raving Loony Party. As one can surmise from the name, the group isn't entirely serious. Founded in 1983 by musician David Sutch (a.k.a. Screaming Lord Sutch), it has offered candidates for numberless elections, from seats in Parliament to the lowliest local posts. Their platform has, at various times, included a call to abolish the income tax; to retrain police officers "too stupid" to do their jobs as vicars in the Church of England; and to require passports for pets.

Ironically, this last idea was taken up by the actual political parties and adopted.

There's little chance of them following the Loony's decision to put an animal in charge, however. In 1999, after Screaming Lord Sutch's suicide, the faithful gathered at the Golden Lion Hotel in Ashburton, Devon, to select a new leader. According to Loony lore, the vote produced a tie between acting chairman Howling Laud Hope and his pet. By general acclamation, he and Cat Mandu became joint leaders.

The feline performed his duties with distinction. He even produced the party's 2001 political manifesto—a blank page. Sadly, his career was cut short when, in July 2002, he was run over by a car while crossing the street. Not that the feline flavor of the Official Monster Raving Loony Party has been totally expunged. In 1978, the organization had adopted the leopard as its official Party Animal, which it remains to this day.

SOCKS

THE UNOFFICIAL MASCOT OF
THE CLINTON ADMINISTRATION

While plenty of U.S. presidents have brought along dogs during their White House tenures, only a handful deigned to keep cats. Bill Clinton joined that short list in 1993 when the family feline, Socks, accompanied the first family to Washington, D.C. It was the culmination of an incredible rags-to-riches story for the black and white mixed breed. Born in 1991, he spent his kittenhood living under the porch of Chelsea Clinton's music teacher's home in Little Rock, Arkansas. The teacher wasn't able to get close to either Socks or his sibling, a kitten named Midnight. But when Chelsea saw the duo and approached them, Socks jumped into her arms.

Thus a media phenomenon was born. Midnight also found a good home, but Socks won worldwide fame. First he lived in the governor's mansion. Then, after Clinton's election to the presidency, the Arkansas tomcat moved to the White House. Instead of crouching under a porch, he spent his days lazing in the garden outside the Oval Office or napping in a favorite chair in the West Wing. He also made numerous public appearances, often traveling in a cat carrier fitted with the presidential seal.

Not that life in a media fishbowl was always perfect. Photographers swarmed Socks, sometimes bribing him with catnip. After it was deemed too dangerous to give him free run of the White House grounds, he was confined to a very long leash. But those inconveniences paled in comparison to his longstanding quarrel with the "first dog," a purebred Labrador retriever named Buddy. According to Hillary Clinton, Socks hated the exuberant canine "instantly and forever." The two did, however, bury the hatchet long enough to pose for the cover of a book called *Dear Socks, Dear Buddy: Kids' Letters to the First Pets.*

After the end of the Clinton administration, Socks received not only a change of address, but a change of family. Given his well-known dislike for Buddy, Socks was turned over to the care of Betty Curie, Bill Clinton's former personal secretary. The cat and Curie had always been great friends, and the Clintons felt that they should enjoy their retirements together. Today she and Socks live in Maryland in a Labrador-free house, far from the limelight.

COLBY

THE CAT WHO WENT
TO COLLEGE, SORT OF

Most people think there's no substitute for a quality education. But in fact there is, as a six-year-old cat named Colby Nolan taught the world. In 2004, Pennsylvania Attorney General Jerry Pappert became aware of a Texas-based diploma mill that sold online college degrees via unsolicited e-mails. To foil the people behind it, his department set up a unique sting operation.

Undercover operatives made online contact with an "institution of higher learning" called Trinity Southern University in Plano, Texas. Actually, TSU didn't exist. But then, neither did Colby Nolan, the eager scholar whom the sting operators claimed to be. According to their e-mails, young Colby was interested in obtaining a bachelor's degree in business administration for the low, low price of $299.

When the TSU representatives sent him a "student application" to fill out, it was returned containing information that shouldn't have qualified him for a GED, let alone university admission. Colby's trumped-up resume stated that he'd taken three community college courses, worked at a fast-food restaurant, and had a paper route. Yet surprisingly (or, perhaps, not so surprisingly), the school's administrators stated that his work experience qualified him not for a bachelor's degree, but for an executive MBA (available for only $399, plus shipping).

The TSU people couldn't know it, but Colby was even more unqualified than his resume made him sound. He was, in fact, a six-year-old black cat belonging to an attorney general's office staffer. Yet once the check for his diploma cleared, he received an authentic-looking sheepskin, complete with signatures from the university's president and dean. Another $99 netted Colby's transcript. It stated that the feline, who could neither speak, read, nor write, and had never set one paw in a classroom, had accumulated a 3.5 GPA.

This was more than enough for the cops. Colby the student was revealed to be Colby the cat, and he even posed for news photographers while wearing a tiny, feline-sized graduation cap. Shortly thereafter charges were filed against the quasi-mythical TSU, along with the individuals who ran it. Not surprisingly, the school's Web site almost immediately vanished from the Internet. All thanks to the school's most notorious graduate.

LEWIS

THE CAT WHO WAS SLAPPED WITH A RESTRAINING ORDER

Some felines become famous, but some become infamous. Such is the case for a longhaired black and white Connecticut tomcat named Lewis. The tiny miscreant's violent temper got him in trouble with the law, earning him what amounts to a life sentence. The formerly outdoor cat has been condemned by city officials in the town of Fairfield to spend the rest of his days indoors—or else. City hall accomplished this by serving him with what was arguably the first restraining order ever issued for a cat; it is certainly the most controversial, widely publicized one.

Lewis's brush with the law began when he launched unprovoked assaults on the people living on a quiet cul-de-sac named Sunset Circle. He appeared out of nowhere, attacking his victims from behind. "He looks like Felix the Cat and has six toes on each foot, each with a long claw," one harassed resident told the *Connecticut Post*. "They are formidable weapons." Lewis apparently wasn't shy about deploying them against anyone who crossed his path, including a hapless Avon lady who was reportedly savaged as she got out of her car.

Finally a neighbor, Janet Kettman, who claimed to have been attacked twice, called the Fairfield

Police Department's animal control officer, Rachel Solveira. The officer slapped a restraining order on the offending beast, which had been dubbed the "Terrorist of Sunset Circle." Lewis was allowed limited outdoor privileges if he took Prozac twice a day. But after a couple of months he was back in hot water when his owner, Ruth Cisero, stopped giving the cat his medication. And then, for good measure, she let him escape from the house. Not surprisingly, his first order of business was to seek out and savage another neighbor, Maureen Bachtig.

In no time, Cisero found herself sharing her pet's punishment. She was arrested for failing to comply with a restraining order and second-degree reckless endangerment, and she was placed on probation. To add insult to injury, one of Lewis's previous victims filed a $5,000 lawsuit against her.

Just when things couldn't get any stranger, they did. The local newspapers broke the story, which quickly exploded into an international media sensation. Smelling a colorful human interest piece, press from around the world fell upon the juicy item like, well, Lewis going after an Avon lady. Overnight, Cisero, her embattled neighbors, and anyone else with the vaguest connection to the cat started fielding calls from everyone from CNN to *Inside Edition* to *The Daily Show* to the BBC. Lewis got his own page on myspace.com, and Save Lewis T-shirts hit the market shortly thereafter.

Cisero dutifully talked to the legions of reporters in hopes that all the interest might somehow help both her case and her cat. As for Lewis, he lounged indoors with his owner's other feline, Thomas, and occasionally posed menacingly for cringing photographers. When he wasn't doing "interviews," he stared forlornly out the window at the birds and squirrels he'd formerly hunted. He was, at least, mercifully oblivious to the high-stakes legal wrangling over his future. In April 2006, at a court appearance crowded with media, Cisero asked for an end to her probation. The judge said she would only consider it if Lewis were euthanized. Finally, in June 2006, Cisero was

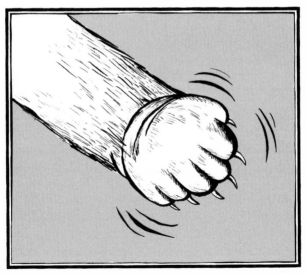

granted "accelerated probation," but with one stipulation. The judge in the case stated that Lewis could never go outside again. "There are no exceptions," she warned sternly. "None."

At last report, Lewis was grudgingly adjusting to house arrest. And his neighbors were reveling in his absence.

OTHER FELINES OF DISTINCTION

SLIPPERS: The arrogant pet of U.S. President Theodore Roosevelt. During a state banquet, an entire procession of diplomats had to detour around the cat, who had fallen asleep in a hallway.

TOM KITTEN: The pet of U.S. President John F. Kennedy's daughter, Caroline. Unfortunately, Kennedy proved allergic to the cat, who was found a new home. At an auction of Jacqueline Kennedy Onassis's estate, a framed picture of Tom sold for a breathtaking $13,000.

MYOBU NO OMOTO: Favored pet of Japanese emperor Ichijo (980–1011). The pampered feline was so exalted that the emperor imprisoned the owner of a dog who dared to chase her.

MICETTO: A large tabby cat born in the Vatican who became the favored pet of Pope Leo XII. The pope allegedly held audiences while Micetto hid in his robes.

WHITE HEATHER: A fat Angora who was Queen Victoria's favorite cat. The cat managed to outlive the famously long-lived queen and became the property of her son and successor, King Edward VII.

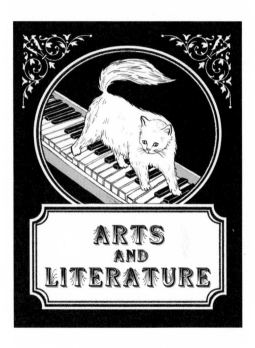

ARTS
AND
LITERATURE

THE HERMITAGE GUARDS

THE CATS WHO WATCH OVER RUSSIA'S GREATEST MUSEUM

Cats have always been great friends of libraries and museums. Because mice and rats will chew up an important old manuscript or a priceless painting just as readily as they would an ear of corn, numerous cultural centers have employed feline assassins to keep vermin damage to a minimum. But few such groups are as ancient, as numerous, or of such regal ancestry as the feline army defending the State Hermitage Museum in Saint Petersburg, Russia.

Today a force of roughly fifty cats watches over the sprawling complex, just as they have for more than two and a half centuries. Their work began back in the days when the Hermitage was still a palace for the czars. In 1745 Peter the Great's daughter, Empress Elizaveta Petrovna, decided she'd had enough of the rodents in the building. She issued a royal proclamation decreeing the roundup of "better cats, the largest ones, able to catch mice." They were to be dispatched to the court, accompanied by someone who could look after them.

The first contingent of felines arrived shortly thereafter. They must have done their work well, because they remained through the reign of every czar. They also survived the communist revolution intact, though the descendants of the original band were decimated during World War II. Saint Petersburg (then called Leningrad) was blockaded for months by German troops. Food became very scarce, and many of the Hermitage cats became entrées.

After the war, their numbers were replenished. While the cats the czars kept were said to be Persians, today's collection is a somewhat motley assortment of former strays domiciled in the building's basement. Donations by employees and proceeds from an annual sale of paintings made by the children of Hermitage workers are used to pay for the cats' medical care, shelter, and food to supplement whatever they catch on their own.

Though the felines regularly patrol outdoors, they're no longer allowed in the galleries and exhibit halls. On rare occasions, however, some do find their way in. But since they usually trigger the museum's elaborate electronic security system in the process, they're promptly escorted right back out.

SELIMA

THE CAT WHO DIED
FOR ART'S SAKE

Many cats enjoy posthumous honors, but few have been commemorated so artfully, or in such varied mediums, as Selima, the companion of eighteenth-century British author, politician, and aristocrat Horace Walpole, fourth Earl of Orford. Perhaps she received so much attention because she died so colorfully. While attempting to reach some goldfish in a porcelain vase, Selima fell in and drowned.

Walpole was bereft. He had an inscription about the cat carved on the offending vase (which can still be seen at his mansion, Strawberry Fields), and asked a poet friend, Thomas Gray, to author an epitaph. Gray went him one better, composing *Ode on the Death of a Favourite Cat*. It advises the reader against striving blindly for unworthy goals, and it ends with the line that has made it immortal: "Not all that tempts your wand'ring eyes / And heedless hearts is lawful prize. / Nor all that glitters, gold."

As if this weren't enough of a monument, in 1776 the artist Stephen Elmer executed a painting called *Horace Walpole's Favourite Cat*, showing Selima perched precariously over the goldfish bowl. Nearby sits a book, opened to Gray's *Ode*.

BEERBOHM

THE CAT WHO UPSTAGED BRITAIN'S FINEST THESPIANS

For centuries no self-respecting English theater—at least, none that wished to be free of vermin—could do without a cat. But besides hunting mice, these felines came to serve other functions. Actors considered them good luck charms, and their calming presence cured many a bout of stage fright. They grew so useful that even the most egotistical performers overlooked the fact that the cats occasionally wandered onstage during productions, upstaging their human associates.

No modern theater cat served as ably, as famously, or as long as Beerbohm, who handled vermin suppression duties at the Gielgud Theatre (formerly the Globe) in London's West End from the 1970s to the early 1990s. The regal-looking tabby often picked certain actors to fawn over, and he wandered onto the boards at least once during the run of every show. Named after British stage veteran Herbert Beerbohm Tree, he worked in show business for twenty years before retiring to Kent to live with the company's carpenter. He died in March 1995—a sad passing that was honored with a front-page obituary in the theater newspaper *The Stage*. His portrait still hangs in the Gielgud.

HODGE

THE CAT WHO HELPED
WRITE A DICTIONARY

Many a famous poet or novelist has written under the languid gaze of a feline. But few such four-legged muses can match the grit and staying power of a black cat named Hodge. He provided companionship to lexicographer Samuel Johnson (1709–1784) as he single-handedly composed the first truly authoritative dictionary of the English language.

Johnson gave eleven years to the work, churning out definition after definition at his home at 17 Gough Square in London. As the great lexicographer labored at his desk, Hodge was often at his elbow, amusing and diverting his owner from what must have been an unimaginable grind. The project was finally completed in 1775. It won universal acclaim, became the literary world's reference of choice for more than a century, and earned its author the nickname "Dictionary Johnson."

However, the world knows about Hodge (and his master) not because of the dictionary, but because of a young Scotsman named James Boswell. Boswell befriended Johnson in 1763 and spent the next few decades following him around, scribbling down the sage's comments and making no secret of his desire to write the great man's biography. In

1799, he duly produced *The Life of Samuel Johnson*, considered the first truly well-rounded, sympathetic, modern biography. It made Johnson, who might have merited no more than a footnote in the history books, into an immortal literary character.

Boswell also turned Hodge into a famous literary cat, despite being pathologically afraid of him. "I never shall forget the indulgence with which he treated Hodge, his cat: for whom he himself used to go out and buy oysters, lest the servants having that trouble should take a dislike to the poor creature," Boswell wrote in *The Life of Johnson*. "I am, unluckily, one of those who have an antipathy to a cat, so that I am uneasy when in the room with one; and I own, I frequently suffered a good deal from the presence of this same Hodge. I recollect him one day scrambling up Dr. Johnson's breast, apparently with much satisfaction, while my friend smiling and half-whistling, rubbed down his back, and pulled him by the tail; and when I observed he was a fine cat, saying, 'Why yes, Sir, but I have had cats whom I liked better than this'; and then as if perceiving Hodge to be out of countenance, adding, 'but he is a very fine cat, a very fine cat indeed.'"

Johnson supported his four-legged companion to the bitter end. Boswell notes how the great lexicographer, as his cat's final hours approached, went off to purchase some valerian (a relative of catnip) to ease his suffering. Upon his death the poet Percival Stockdale wrote *An Elegy on the Death of Dr Johnson's Favourite Cat*, which reads in part, "Who, by his master when caressed / Warmly his gratitude expressed / And never failed his thanks to purr / Whene'er he stroked his sable fur."

Today, across the street from the building where Johnson composed his masterwork, stands a statue of Hodge perched atop a copy of his owner's book. In his dictionary, Johnson defined cats in general as "a domestic animal that catches mice, commonly reckoned by naturalists the lowest order of the leonine species." But it is his more gracious assessment of Hodge, as "a very fine cat indeed," that adorns the statue of his literary soul mate.

CATTARINA
THE CAT WHO TOUCHED THE DARK HEART OF POE

During his short literary career, Edgar Allan Poe wrote great poems, penned some of the world's most terrifying horror stories, and invented the detective novel. But his achievements brought him neither happiness nor material success. Quite the contrary. Before his death from alcohol abuse in 1849 at age forty, he suffered more than a lifetime's worth of disappointment, rejection, and grief.

In 1842, his wife, Virginia, was diagnosed with tuberculosis. For the next five years, until her death in 1847, her health deteriorated. The couple's poverty exacerbated her suffering. Poe, though intermittently employed at various magazines, was never well off. And his personal demons, chiefly his inability to stop drinking, brought turmoil to his home. His problem grew so severe that he feared he might actually hurt Virginia during one of his drunken fits.

Throughout these years the couple's most devoted companion was a feline named Cattarina. The Poes, who didn't stand on ceremony, sometimes called their tortoiseshell cat Kate (Poe himself was often referred to as "Eddie"). The cat would sit on her master's shoulder as he wrote and would cuddle next to Virginia, sometimes providing

the only warmth that their freezing cottage had to offer.

Poe never physically harmed his wife, who by all accounts he loved deeply. But the fear was always there, along with what must have been searing guilt over his inability to give her a better life. He shared those feelings of inadequacy and self-loathing in his story *The Black Cat*—a tale of unparalleled gruesomeness inspired in part by Cattarina's devotion to Virginia and by Poe's anxiety about his own dark side.

The story, written in 1842, tells the tale of a drunk who, in a fit of alcoholic rage, hangs his cat, who Poe describes as a "beautiful animal, entirely black, and sagacious to an astonishing degree." Not long afterward he's followed home by another feline that looks almost exactly like the one he killed—except for an unnerving ring of white fur around the creature's neck.

The man's wife takes an immediate liking to the newcomer, and they become inseparable. The man, however, comes to believe that his new pet wants to avenge his earlier crime. During yet another drunken rage he tries to kill it with an ax, only to murder his wife instead. He quickly walls up her body in the basement and is relieved to find that the cat has disappeared.

Later, he brazenly shows the basement to searchers sent to investigate his wife's disappearance. But suddenly, a terrible wail erupts from behind the masonry. The wall is pulled down, revealing the dead woman with the black cat perched on her head, screeching. In his haste the man had sealed up the animal with his wife.

The story's finale is one of the most unforgettable scenes in horror literature—and one of the most psychologically revealing. In the real world, Poe tried his best to care for his wife, and never gave so much as a dirty look to his dark muse, Cattarina. But it probably crossed his mind that this tortoiseshell feline served his wife better and more faithfully than he ever managed to. If so, then perhaps *The Black Cat* accomplished two things: It cast the fears and inadequacies of its author into sharp relief, and it honored the memory of the selfless Cattarina, whose literary incarnation has outlived both herself, her mistress, and her master.

PANGUR BAN
IRELAND'S MOST FAMOUS FELINE

For most of history, the only way to create a new copy of an old book was to obtain a stack of fresh parchment, pull up a chair, break out a pot of ink, and laboriously copy every line by hand. During the Middle Ages this mind-numbing task was raised to an art form by Catholic monks, legions of whom spent their lives huddled over tables in stone cells all over Europe, copying everything from Greek and Roman classics to the latest papal pronouncements. Much of the knowledge that survived from ancient times did so only because of their unceasing efforts.

Working as a scribe was important, but not very creative. That's why so few of these human photocopy machines made any sort of mark on history. One of that handful was a young man who, sometime in the ninth century, perhaps trained as a student copyist at the Monastery of St Paul in Carinthia, Austria. We don't know his name, but thanks to a short poem he scribbled on the back of a copy of St Paul's Epistles, we do know the name of his cat—Pangur Ban.

That feline, apparently, was the medieval manuscript copier's bosom friend. The young Irishman (his origin is known because the poem was written in Gaelic) traveled all the way from the Emerald

Isle to Austria to acquire the skills of a scribe. There he must have spent endless days and nights in relative isolation, his only company the manuscript he was working on and his faithful white cat, Pangur Ban. Again, scholars can guess at the feline's color because in Gaelic *ban* means "white." This man, who was obviously a long way from home, decided, for reasons unknown, to slip among the monastery's weighty manuscripts a short poem about his relationship with his cat. Reading it now (in a translation by Robin Flower), one can almost hear the feline frisking around the lonely monk's cell as he works:

I and Pangur Ban, my cat,
'Tis a like task we are at;
Hunting mice is his delight,
Hunting words I sit all night.

Better far than praise of men
'Tis to sit with book and pen;
Pangur bears me no ill will,
He too plies his simple skill.

'Tis a merry thing to see
At our tasks how glad are we,
When at home we sit and find
Entertainment to our mind.

Oftentimes a mouse will stray

In the hero Pangur's way;
Oftentimes my keen thought set
Takes a meaning in its net.

'Gainst the wall he sets his eye
Full and fierce and sharp and sly;
'Gainst the wall of knowledge I
All my little wisdom try.

When a mouse darts from its den,
O how glad is Pangur then!
O what gladness do I prove
When I solve the doubts I love!

So in peace our tasks we ply,
Pangur Ban, my cat, and I;
In our arts we find our bliss,
I have mine and he has his.

Practice every day has made
Pangur perfect in his trade;
I get wisdom day and night
Turning darkness into light.

No one will ever learn the ultimate fate of either the poetic monk or his cat. And of course, he can never know that his poem, authored perhaps in a moment of fatigue or whimsy, would leave its mark on history. Found centuries later, the little ditty became one of the greatest examples of early Irish poetry.

PETER

THE CAT WHO DROVE
HIS MASTER NUTS

One of the most famous illustrators of the late nineteenth and early twentieth centuries was an Englishman named Louis Wain. He made his fortune drawing fanciful pictures of anthropomorphized cats doing everything from playing golf to having tea. This feline version of the dogs-playing-poker franchise was inspired by Wain's own pet, Peter.

Sadly, Wain's cat pictures provide a riveting visual record of his eventual descent into madness. Born August 5, 1860, Wain began his artistic career as a teen. During his early twenties he worked as a freelancer of modest reputation. Then his wife, Emily, began a long struggle with cancer, which would eventually claim her life. Since she took great solace from their black and white cat, Peter, Wain taught him tricks, such as wearing spectacles. Then he started drawing the cat in more fanciful situations, and a new career was born. "To him properly belongs the foundation of my career, the developments of my initial efforts, and the establishing of my work," he wrote.

For years thereafter, Peter would be seen again and again in his master's renderings. In 1886, Wain drew a massive piece called *A Kitten's Christmas Party* for the *Illustrated London News*. It won him wide acclaim, and soon his pictures of upright-walking, clothes-wearing cats were everywhere. It's hard to overestimate Wain's popularity. His felines graced everything from greeting cards to children's books to the *Louis Wain Annual*, a magazine devoted to his caricatures. He was to cats what Thomas Kinkade is to cottages.

Sadly, though the artist's work is still remembered today, it is for a darker reason. Late in life Wain developed schizophrenia and spent almost two decades confined to mental hospitals before his death in 1939. He painted until the end, unwittingly creating a disturbing record of his descent into madness. As his schizophrenia took hold, the clothes-wearing cats disappeared. Instead Wain created ever more abstract-looking feline portraits, with the subjects rendered in bright, almost psychedelic colors and sporting surprised, even terrified, expressions. In his final works—basically collections of small, geometric shapes—the "cats" are merely complex kaleidoscopic patterns. And yet, even toward the end, the poor mad artist occasionally created portraits that looked like Peter, the cat who started it all.

MASTER'S CAT

THE CAT WHO CHARMED
THE DICKENS OUT OF DICKENS

English novelist Charles Dickens was a great fan of dogs and birds—so fond, in fact, that for years cats were banned from his London household, lest they make off with his feathered friends. But all that changed when Dickens's daughter, Mamie, received a white kitten as a gift. The cat was christened William. Shortly thereafter, after giving birth to kittens, she was rechristened Williamina.

The feline family was supposed to stay in a box in the kitchen. But Williamina had other plans. One by one she carried her kittens into Dickens's study and deposited them in a corner. Dickens told his daughter that they couldn't stay and had her take them back to the kitchen. But Williamina brought them back. Mamie removed them again, only to have the mother once more laboriously haul them into the study. Only this time she laid them directly at the great man's feet and then stared at him imploringly, as if begging permission to stay.

It was finally granted, and the kittens enjoyed the privilege of climbing up the curtains and scampering across Dickens's desk as he tried to work. When they were old enough, all were found good homes—except for a single deaf kitten.

Because it could never hear its name, it was never given one. Instead he was known simply as "the master's cat." And indeed he was. He followed Dickens like a dog throughout the house and would sit by him at his desk as he wrote.

Not that the master's cat didn't demand a certain level of attention from the master. One night, when the rest of his family went out to attend a ball, Dickens sat in his study by a candle, engrossed in a book. The cat, as usual, was at his side. Suddenly the candle flickered out. Dickens, too engrossed in his reading to notice the cause, relit the candle and continued. He also gave a passing pat on the head to his cat, who stared at him longingly.

A minute or two later, the candle flickered again. Dickens looked up just in time to see his companion deliberately trying to put out the flame with his paw. The author set his book aside and played with the cat, then shared the story with his family the next day.

HAMLET

THE CAT WHO HELD COURT OVER A LITERARY ROUND TABLE

For decades, Manhattan's elegant Algonquin Hotel has been a gathering place for the city's theater crowd and literati. But during its heyday, its greatest celebrity arguably wasn't Dorothy Parker or Robert Benchley but a scraggly former stray cat named Hamlet.

According to legend, the feline, originally called Rusty, was an unemployed theater cat taken in by the hotel's owner, Frank Case. It must have been quite a step up. The old tomcat was renamed Hamlet and given the run of the hotel. He even got his own cat door to ease his travels and is said to have enjoyed lapping milk from a champagne glass. When he passed away after only three years on the job, the *New York Times* noted his departure in its gossip column.

Though the original Hamlet is a distant memory, the tradition of keeping a cat at the Algonquin lives on. Today the position is held by a former animal shelter inmate named Matilda. Like her predecessors, she has the run of the place (save for the kitchen and hotel dining room) and receives fan mail from around the world.

PULCINELLA
THE CAT WHO WROTE A FUGUE

Today the name Domenico Scarlatti doesn't exactly fall trippingly off the tongues of music aficionados. In the early eighteenth century, however, the Italian-born composer was famous throughout Europe. A master of the keyboard, he commanded respect both from his contemporaries and successors. He was considered George Frederic Handel's equal on the harpsichord. Artists ranging from Chopin to Brahms to Vladimir Horowitz have idolized his work for centuries, but he was also extremely popular with lay audiences.

He was as prolific as he was skilled. During his lifetime (1685–1757) he created several operas and produced some five hundred sonatas, all while holding various high-profile musical posts in Italy, England, Portugal, and Spain, where he lived for more than two decades. Scarlatti became famous not just for his intricate, innovative keyboard pieces, but also for his somewhat unorthodox style, which sampled everything from religious themes to Spanish, Moorish, and Jewish folk music. But one of his most famous pieces was inspired not by some rustic melody or the work of another composer. It was a collaboration with his cat. Officially called the Fugue in G minor, Kk. 30, this one-

movement harpsichord sonata is unofficially known as the Cat's Fugue.

According to legend, the maestro owned a cat named Pulcinella, who enjoyed walking up and down the keyboard of his harpsichord. Usually this produced only random, meaningless noise. But during one of these "improvisation sessions," the feline plinked out an unusual, though quite catchy, series of notes. Scarlatti grabbed a pad and wrote down the short phrase. Inspired, he composed an entire fugue around it.

The piece became an instant success, and it remains so today. During the 1840s, the great pianist Franz Liszt added the work to his repertoire—it became a regular part of his performances. By that time a major oversight on Scarlatti's part had been rectified. At the time he wrote it, the idea of somehow noting the origin of the piece in the title simply didn't occur to him. But by the early nineteenth century the brilliant bit of feline-inspired music had become universally known as the Cat's Fugue.

CALVIN

THE CAT WHO INSPIRED TWO AUTHORS

It is the rarest of literary cats who serves as the muse of not one but two writers. Such was the case for a fluffy Maltese named Calvin. He entered the world of letters in the mid-nineteenth century, when he wandered "out of the great unknown" into the household of Harriet Beecher Stowe. "It was as if he had inquired at the door if this was the residence of the author of *Uncle Tom's Cabin*, and, upon being assured that it was, had decided to dwell there," remarked family friend Charles Dudley Warner. Calvin immediately made himself at home. He hovered nearby as Stowe wrote, sometimes even perching on her shoulders. All were impressed not only by the feline's self-confidence, but by his intelligence. "He is a reasonable cat and understands pretty much everything except binomial theorem," said Warner.

He was in a unique position to know. When Stowe decamped from her New England home to Florida, custody of Calvin was awarded to him. The cat prowled his Connecticut estate for eight years. "He would sit quietly in my study for hours, then, moved by a delicate affection, come and pull at my sleeve until he could touch my face with his nose, and then go away contented," Warner wrote.

He could also open doors on his own and open register vents when he felt cold. According to his owner, Calvin seemed equal to almost any challenge, save for one: "He could do almost any thing but speak, and you would declare sometimes that you could see a pathetic longing to do that in his intelligent face."

Calvin became such a part of the family that, when the feline finally passed away, he received a long, loving eulogy in the author's bestselling collection of 1871 essays, *My Summer in a Garden*. The elegy, called *Calvin (A Study of Character)*, became nationally famous. "I have set down nothing concerning him but the literal truth," Warner wrote. "He was always a mystery. I did not know whence he came. I do not know whither he has gone. I would not weave one spray of falsehood in the wreath I lay upon his grave."

The pint-sized literary lion who loved the world of letters had now become a part of it forever.

DINAH

THE SECOND-MOST-FAMOUS CAT
IN ALICE IN WONDERLAND

Ask the typical reader to name the feline star of the Lewis Carroll books *Alice's Adventures in Wonderland* and *Through the Looking Glass*, and he or she will likely mention the Cheshire Cat. But another cat plays an important role in the two works. It's a cat who, like so many characters in the books, was based in reality.

Carroll, whose real name was Charles Lutwidge Dodgson, first spun the tale during a lazy afternoon boat trip down the Thames River with a friend, Robinson Duckworth, and three little girls of whom he was particularly fond: Lorina, Alice, and Edity Liddell. The three enjoyed the story so much that Alice, the tale's namesake, asked Dodgson to write it down. He did, showed the draft to friends, and was encouraged to find a publisher. The first of the two books, *Alice's Adventures in Wonderland*, was published on July 4, 1865. It became an immediate sensation and has remained in print ever since.

For a tale of fantasy, the book includes a great many thinly disguised real people. The protagonist is, of course, Alice Liddell. Robinson Duckworth becomes the Duck, and Carroll himself becomes the Dodo (perhaps because he stuttered, which caused his real last name to often come out as Do-Do-Dodgson). As for pets, the book's Alice talks repeatedly about Dinah, Alice Liddell's real tortoiseshell tabby. Interestingly, the references form one of the dark, rather sadistic veins that flow through the text.

Whenever poor Dinah comes up in conversation, it's always in the context of thoughtless cruelty. For instance, early in *Wonderland*, Alice mentions how her pet is "such a capital one for catching mice," apparently forgetting that she's conversing with a talking mouse at the time. And later, in *Looking Glass*, she makes the same sort of faux pas when addressing a group of birds. "Dinah's our cat," she says. "And she's such a capital one for catching mice you can't think! And oh, I wish you could see her after the birds! Why, she'll eat a little bird as soon as look at it!" No wonder Alice got into so much trouble in Wonderland.

FOSS

THE CAT WHO WAS ALMOST
TOO GOOD TO BE TRUE

The cats of great artists and writers often find themselves immortalized in their masters' works. But in the strange case of nineteenth-century British artist and writer Edward Lear, a bit of poetic whimsy seems to have found its way into the real world.

The bearded, bespectacled eccentric gained fame as a painter of animals and landscapes. But he also published several books of children's nonsense poems that made him internationally famous. Many, including *The Owl and the Pussycat*, are still read to toddlers today.

Lear illustrated his poems with lighthearted cartoons. One of his favorite subjects was a striped tomcat named Foss, who he acquired in 1872. Lear's devotion to his pet is quite amazing, considering that Foss was by all accounts a most unattractive subject. He was fat, with a bobbed tail reportedly cut off by a superstitious servant who believed it would stop him from roaming. Yet there's no end to the pictures Lear drew of himself and his rotund friend on adventures. No photos exist of the famous feline. When Lear tried to take one, the big orange cat jumped out of his master's arms just before the shutter clicked.

Lear loved Foss so much that, when the artist built a new home, he made it look exactly like his old one, so as not to upset the cat. And when Foss passed away in 1887, he was buried in his master's garden under a large memorial stone. Lear himself died only two months later.

Today pictures of Foss can still be seen in collections of Lear's nonsense poems. But there's something mysterious about them. The *real* Foss didn't enter the artist's life until 1872. Yet years earlier he regularly produced drawings of a similar fat, striped, stub-tailed cat. And for some reason, Lear was convinced that Foss lived a near-impossible thirty-one years—so much so that he had that figure carved on his friend's tombstone. Perhaps he saw the real Foss as the incarnation of the imaginary cat he'd carried in his mind's eye for decades. "Edward adored Foss, and it was mutual, but the Foss we know belongs more to the world of nonsense stories than he does to the real world," says Lear biographer Peter Levi. Maybe he always did.

COBBY

THE CAT WHO STOLE HIS MASTER'S HEART—LITERALLY

After the death of English poet and novelist Thomas Hardy on January 11, 1928, his pet cat, Cobby, reportedly vanished, never to be seen again. This strange occurrence gave rise to one of the most macabre stories in the history of Western literature.

It began shortly after the great man's passing, when a contest broke out over where to bury his body. Hardy's will stated explicitly that he wanted to be laid to rest with minimal ceremony in his hometown of Stinsford. However, the executor of his will thought that the author of such classics as *Tess of the d'Urbervilles*, *The Mayor of Casterbridge*, and *The Return of the Native* should enjoy more august accommodations. Specifically, he wanted Hardy to find repose in the fabled Poet's Corner of Westminster Abbey, near such luminaries as Charles Dickens, Geoffrey Chaucer, and Dr. Samuel Johnson.

After heated debate with the family, a compromise was reached: Hardy's body would go to Westminster Abbey and his heart to Stinsford. This would require a bit of postmortem surgery—a job that Hardy's personal physician reportedly declined to undertake. Another doctor was found, and the organ was removed while the great author lay in state at his home. Tradition says it was wrapped in a tea cloth, placed in a biscuit tin, and set aside for transport.

According to one version of the story, the next day the undertaker charged with carrying the heart to Stinsford discovered the box was empty and Cobby was nowhere to be found—the assumption being, of course, that the cat ran off with his owner's heart. But there's an even more horrifying telling of the tale. Some contend that, on the fateful day, authorities found the box empty save for a few scraps of flesh—and that Cobby sat nearby, washing the blood off his muzzle.

In this version of the story, the undertaker came up with a rough-and-ready solution. He had to bury the heart. The heart was inside Cobby. So he throttled the poor cat and secretly interred him at Stinsford. How much of the story is true? Only an inspection of the grave's contents could answer that question. But what is known for sure is that poor Cobby was never seen again.

POLAR BEAR

THE CAT WHO CHARMED
A CURMUDGEON

Cleveland Amory was a well-known literary figure throughout his life. He was the youngest-ever editor at the *Saturday Evening Post*, chief critic for *TV Guide*, and the author of such bestsellers as *The Proper Bostonians* and *Who Killed Society?* But it took a New York City tomcat to turn him into a household name.

It happened on Christmas Eve 1977, when Amory, an avowed dog person, helped rescue an injured stray cat lurking in an alley near his apartment. The cat rewarded his effort by slashing him across both hands. Nevertheless, Amory adopted him. He discovered, while bathing the extraordinarily dirty creature, that it was snow white. Accordingly, he named him Polar Bear.

The two became fast friends, and the cat became an invaluable partner in Amory's long-running crusade for animal rights. Over the years Amory had done everything from cofounding the Humane Society of the United States to launching the Fund for Animals, dedicated to protecting rare and endangered wildlife. Those causes received an enormous boost in 1988, when he published a book about his life with Polar Bear called *The Cat Who Came for Christmas*. It rocketed to No. 1 on the *New York Times* bestseller list, as did its two sequels, *The Cat and the Curmudgeon* and *The Best Cat Ever*.

The works turned Polar Bear into a celebrity among cat fans and animal rights activists. He was even invited to become ship's cat aboard the Greenpeace vessel *Sea Shepherd* (an offer that Amory, on his pet's behalf, respectfully declined). Perhaps most importantly, he cast light on his owner's animal rights work, including a scheme to airlift burros out of the Grand Canyon to save them from government culling and an effort to paint seal pups with harmless dyes to make their pelts worthless to trappers.

The two parted ways in 1991, when Polar Bear passed away. He was buried at Black Beauty Ranch, a Texas refuge established by the Fund for Animals to care for abused and abandoned creatures. His memorial reads, "Beneath these stones lie the mortal remains of The Cat Who Came for Christmas, Beloved Polar Bear. 'Til we meet again." They met again when Amory, who died in 1998, was laid to rest beside him.

MYSOUFF II

THE CAT WHO ATE THE CANARIES

French novelist Alexandre Dumas, the author of such classics as *The Three Musketeers*, *The Man in the Iron Mask*, and *The Count of Monte Cristo*, was famous for his high living and bizarre exploits. So when his cat, Mysouff II, displeased him, he was given a punishment perfectly in keeping with his owner's imaginative nature. Luckily for him, it was too imaginative to execute.

Mysouff II was actually the second cat in this feline dynasty. The original Mysouff had been at Dumas' side when he was just starting out as a writer. Every day the feline would see his master off to work, and every evening he met Dumas at the corner to escort him home. The cat would unerringly meet him at the same spot, even if he arrived before or after his usual time.

After the passing of this faithful original came Mysouff II, a black and white shorthaired feline who was discovered in the basement of Dumas' home by a cook. By then the author had become rich and famous, and he lived in luxury. Mysouff II also enjoyed plenty of pampering—until he found a way to mess up a good thing. Among Dumas' many, many indulgences was a collection of monkeys and another of exotic birds that lived on the property. One day the cat found his way into the aviary and proceeded to consume the entire flock.

Dumas was horrified, but also somewhat amused. He decided to put the offending feline on trial for the crime. The next Sunday he argued the case before a handpicked "jury" of friends. During the trial someone pointed out an extenuating circumstance: The aviary door had been opened by one of the monkeys, and the feline had simply taken advantage of the situation.

Since the simians were clearly implicated as accomplices, Dumas decided that poor Mysouff II should spend the next five years imprisoned with them. But fate spared him from incarceration. Shortly after the cat started serving his sentence, the author suffered a huge financial setback. A round of belt tightening followed, and the expensive monkeys and their cage were put on the auction block. Mysouff II not only got to stay, but also won early parole.

JEOFFREY
THE WORLD'S MOST GODLY CAT

Pity poor Christopher Smart. An English poet born in 1722, Smart began writing award-winning verses during his years as a student at Cambridge University. Sadly, he was also drinking excessively, running up debts, and hiding from creditors. After graduating, he edited and wrote for various London publications, sometimes adopting bizarre pseudonyms such as Mary Midnight. Around 1751, he experienced a religious conversion, which coincided more or less with a descent into madness. He began accosting passersby in London's Hyde Park, demanding that they immediately get down on their knees and pray with him. His odd behavior landed him in a mental asylum from 1756 to 1758.

But perhaps Smart wasn't as irrational as he seemed. While confined at the asylum, he produced some of his best work, including a collection of poems called *A Song of David*. He also authored the exceedingly strange *Jubilante Agno*, a collection of free verse celebrating and cataloging the world's divine architecture. In it he praises—often in excruciating detail—every single blessing he feels God has bestowed upon him. Not surprisingly, the massive work includes a loving tribute to Smart's cat. He lists the feline's attributes in a section appropriately called *For I Will Consider My Cat Jeoffrey*, stating that he is a wonder of creation: "For he is a mixture of gravity and waggery. For he knows that God is his Saviour. For there is nothing sweeter than his peace when at rest. For there is nothing brisker than his life when in motion."

Though Smart emerged from the asylum with his poetic reputation enhanced, the same couldn't be said of his financial or personal affairs. His wife and children were forced to abandon him to avoid poverty, and he died penniless in 1771. Interestingly, his idiosyncratic *Jubilante Agno* wasn't published until 1939. But when it was, his ode to Jeoffrey became an instant favorite with cat lovers worldwide. Apparently more than a few readers saw their own felines in Smart's loving description of his pet.

OTHER FELINES OF DISTINCTION

MINOU: Pet of famous French writer and iconoclast George Sand. They were so close that Sand and the cat supposedly shared breakfast from the same bowl.

TAKI: Pet of Raymond Chandler, father of the hard-boiled detective novel genre and creator of the archetypical gumshoe Philip Marlowe. Chandler read the first drafts of his mysteries to the cat, whom he referred to as his "feline secretary."

PUDLENKA: The pet of Czech playwright Karel Capek. He felt that the female, who arrived on his doorstep shortly after the poisoning death of his previous cat, had been sent to avenge the loss. The female bore twenty-six kittens in her lifetime. Her successor, Pudlenka 2, had twenty-one.

BOSCH AND TOMMY: Two cats, always fighting, who helped keep Anne Frank company while she and her family hid from the Nazis in Amsterdam. Bosch is an ethnic slur applied to Germans; Tommy is slang for a British soldier.

HINSE: A particularly bad-tempered pet of novelist Sir Walter Scott who regularly attacked his master's many hunting dogs. This pastime proved his undoing in 1826, when he was killed by a bloodhound named Nimrod.

POPULAR
CULTURE

PEPPER

THE FIRST FELINE MOVIE STAR

At the dawn of the twentieth century, when the first "flickers" started playing at packed nickelodeons worldwide, it seemed as if almost anyone could step in front of a camera and become a star. All they needed were pluck, luck, and, perhaps, a slightly larger than normal ego. Those were the days when former Shakespearian actors, vaudeville hacks, and even theater stagehands all made fortunes in Hollywood. Even a bedraggled alley cat saw her name up in lights.

Her name was Pepper. According to her press clippings, she was "discovered" by famous comedy director Max Sennet. One day, while the creator of the Keystone Cops was shooting a picture, he noticed that a gray cat had sneaked onto the set through a loose floorboard. Far from causing a scene, she actually shot one. The unflappable feline walked out among the actors as if on cue, emoting as if she'd done it all her life. Sennet, impressed, decided he had a star on his hands. He instantly christened the cat Pepper and put her to work.

Her career spanned the late 1910s to the late 1920s. As it turned out, she was much more than a furry, purring prop. Capable of learning complicated tricks, she convincingly played checkers onscreen with comedian Ben Turpin. Over the years she contributed to a long list of comedy shorts with titles such as *The Kitchen Lady*, *Never Too Old*, and *Rip and Stitch: Tailors*.

She also worked with a truly stellar list of costars. Pepper shared billing with talents ranging from the Keystone Cops to Charlie Chaplin to Fatty Arbuckle. She was even able to restrain her instincts when paired with another of Sennet's furry actors, Frederich the Mouse.

But her favorite costar was a Great Dane named Teddy, who was arguably America's first canine movie hero. Pepper worked with Teddy (a.k.a. Keystone Teddy, America's Best Friend, and Teddy the Wonder Dog) in several of Max Sennet's comedies. The two became inseparable—so much so that when Teddy died in the late '20s, his four-legged friend went into deep mourning. The feline fatale threw in the towel shortly thereafter, retiring from acting to enjoy, one hopes, a well-earned rest on a sunny window ledge.

KASPAR

THE WORLD'S LUCKIEST BLACK CAT

London's famous Savoy Hotel has been the epitome of grace and high style since it opened in 1889. From the start, it made a point of taking care of guests' every need. That's what made the unfortunate events of 1898 so unnerving. One night, a South African businessman named Woolf Joel booked a dinner for fourteen. But at the last minute one guest dropped out, turning it into a decidedly less festive party of thirteen. Of course, Joel was well aware of the old legend that the first person to rise from such an unlucky assembly will meet disaster. He chose to laugh off the danger. In a grand act of gallantry, he took any possible consequences upon himself by exiting first.

It was a brave deed—but perhaps a foolish one. Shortly after his return to South Africa, Joel was found murdered in his office.

Did his dining arrangements that night at the Savoy have anything to do with it? The management elected not to take any chances. For several years thereafter, a staff member would sit in with shorthanded groups, partaking of the meal at the hotel's expense. However, since dining with a stranger could make for awkward table talk, a more permanent solution was developed. In

1927, a three-foot-tall wooden statue of a black cat was commissioned from artist Basil Ionides. The Art Deco sculpture was named Kaspar and deployed to round out lunch and dinner groups that formed an unfortunate baker's dozen.

Since then, Kaspar has become a Savoy celebrity, often requested even by groups of more or less than the fateful thirteen. Like all other lunch and dinner guests, the mute feline has his cutlery and plates replaced with each course. The servers even tie a napkin daintily around his neck.

Over the decades, Kaspar has broken bread with numberless luminaries. The cat was a favorite of Winston Churchill, whose dining society, the Other Club, was born at the Savoy. The great wartime prime minister once had to come to Kaspar's aid, securing his release after he was kidnapped as a prank by some Royal Air Force members. Perhaps Churchill liked him so much because he never, ever, repeated anything he heard at the table.

ORANGEY

THE QUEEN OF THE MOVIE CAMEOS

When one thinks of four-legged actors and actresses, canines generally come to mind. But a handful of cats have also clawed their way to the top. At the summit of this short list of feline thespians proudly perches Orangey, a red tabby "discovered" by legendary animal trainer Frank Inn (whose other pupils included Benji and Arnold, the pig from *Green Acres*). Orangey debuted in 1951 in the forgettable flick *Rhubarb*, which chronicled the story of a cat who inherits a baseball team.

Her later roles, however, were more stellar. In addition to playing Minerva in the 1950s television series *Our Miss Brooks*, she also found time for cameos in a number of well-known big-screen projects, including the science fiction classics *This Island Earth* and *The Incredible Shrinking Man*, in which she tried to chase down and eat the film's diminutive title character. Orangey reached the pinnacle of her fame in 1961, playing opposite Audrey Hepburn as her pet cat, Cat, in *Breakfast at Tiffany's*. In 1952, she received a Patsy Award (the animal world's equivalent of the Oscar) for *Rhubarb*, and in 1962 she crowned her career with another statuette for *Breakfast at Tiffany's*.

MIMSEY

THE CAT WHO MADE FUN
OF LEO THE LION

When Mary Tyler Moore Enterprises (MTM) debuted in the late 1960s, no one knew it would soon create such hits as *The Mary Tyler Moore Show*, *Hill Street Blues*, and *The Bob Newhart Show*. The upstart production company decided to trade on its passing resemblance to the Metro-Goldwyn Mayer (MGM) name to make it's mark. That storied company was represented by a roaring lion. MTM wanted something similar, but since it was a much smaller, younger operation, management picked a much smaller, younger feline mascot—an orange kitten named Mimsey.

The former animal shelter inmate, only a few weeks old, was placed in front of a camera. She uttered a squeaky, uncertain meow, and her TV career was over. She was given to an MTM staffer as a pet.

But her TV incarnation developed a life of its own. The eternal kitten's meow graced the closing credits of every MTM show. Over the decades her appearance was even tailored to fit specific programs. On *Hill Street Blues* she wore a police hat, and on *St. Elsewhere* a surgical mask. The real Mimsey passed on in 1988, but her TV doppelganger remains forever young.

TOWSER

THE WORLD'S MOST SPIRITED MOUSE HUNTER

On the grounds of Scotland's Glenturret Distillery, birthplace of the delectable Famous Grouse whiskey, stands a bronze statue honoring a distinguished former employee. But it doesn't celebrate an owner or a particularly skilled distiller or even a human being. It bears the likeness of a female long-haired tortoiseshell cat named Towser, along with her proud claim to fame: "Towser, the famous cat who lived in the still house, Glenturret Distillery, for almost twenty-four years. She caught 28,899 mice in her lifetime. World mousing champion, *Guinness Book of Records*."

It's no surprise that a distillery needs such a bloody-minded creature. The large amounts of barley stored there attract large numbers of rodents. At Glenturret, as at other distilleries, a feline is the first line of defense. But even among such exceptional company, Towser stood alone. During her very long life, Towser is estimated to have killed three mice every day from shortly after her birth on April 21, 1963, to shortly before her death on March 30, 1987.

This reign of rodent terror made Towser a celebrity. She appeared on television programs, received fan mail, and was much in demand for photo opportunities with distillery visitors. After her death, she was replaced by another cat, Amber. Though Amber was quite happy to greet guests, during her tenure (which lasted until her own demise in 2004) she reportedly never killed a single mouse. Today her duties are performed by a former stray named Brooke, who earned her job in a Scotland-wide talent search. Unfortunately, when it comes to killing rodents, Brooke is no Towser. According to the Glenturret Web site, she's "more usually found curled up on a barrel asleep in the sun than chasing mice." Happily, improved grain storage techniques have drastically reduced the mouse population at Glenturret, leaving Brooke plenty of time for the task at which she truly excels—posing for photo ops with visitors.

How did Towser catch so many mice? Staffers at the distillery wonder if she got an extra boost from her evening saucer of milk, which was fortified with a "tiny wee dram" of the distillery's powerful product. Perhaps she defended the place so well because she knew, from firsthand experience, what she was fighting for.

LUCKY

THE CAT WHO CREATED
AN ADVERTISING CAMPAIGN

Everyone knows Morris the Cat, the spokesfeline for 9 Lives Cat Food. The big orange tabby, who first took to the airwaves back in the '60s, is famous for his jaded voice, blasé worldview, and, of course, his finicky attitude toward every comestible under the sun, save for 9 Lives.

That persona made him an icon. But the real-life feline who portrayed Morris was neither blasé nor finicky. A friendless stray can't afford to be.

The cat selected to play Morris on TV was originally called Lucky. And lucky he was. An inmate at the Hinsdale Humane Society Animal Shelter in Lombard, Illinois, he was only hours away from being euthanized. But shelter officials saw something special in the cat's distinguished good looks and green eyes. In the spring of 1967, they contacted animal trainer Bob Martwick, who was so smitten by the feline that he adopted him.

Springing for Lucky's $5 adoption fee was the best investment Martwick ever made. A few months later he was contacted by the Leo Burnett Advertising Agency, which needed a good-looking cat to eat a bowl of food for a commercial. The product was, of course, 9 Lives. Lucky—soon to be rechristened Morris—wowed the agency's executives, and in June

1969 he debuted on national TV. Almost overnight, an advertising icon was born. Soon bags of fan mail addressed to Morris inundated the 9 Lives headquarters. Even more to the point, mountains of their product flew off of store shelves.

Morris's fame soon spread to other media. He appeared in the 1972 movie *Shamus*; posed for the cover of *Cat Fancy's* thirtieth anniversary issue in 1995; and won back-to-back Patsy Awards (the animal world's equivalent of the Oscar) in 1972 and 1973. He was also offered as a presidential candidate in 1988 and again in 1992.

But while the name and fame of Morris live on, his original alter ego, Lucky, passed away in 1975. Since then he's been played by a string of lookalikes. The current incarnation lives in Los Angeles with his trainer, Rose Ordile. The original Morris, who lived to an estimated age of nineteen, was buried with great ceremony in Martwick's backyard.

THE MEOW MIX CAT

THE CAT WHO ALMOST GAVE HIS LIFE FOR ADVERTISING

In the days before computer-generated special effects, animal trainers used heroic measures to get four-legged thespians to "talk" onscreen. (The only thing that got the famous Mr. Ed to move his mouth on cue was a dose of peanut butter smeared under his upper lip.) But one famous feline pitch cat managed to spontaneously inaugurate one of the world's most recognizable promotional campaigns.

It began in the early 1970s, when the advertising agency Della Femina, Travisano & Partners was engaged to create TV spots for Meow Mix cat food. When they shot footage of an orange-and-white tabby consuming the product, however, the luckless cat started choking. All they got was at-first-unusable footage of the feline working its mouth soundlessly as it fought for air. But then ad exec Jerry Della Femina thought of a way to turn lemons into lemonade. He added a soundtrack to the film, created the now-immortal "Meow, meow, meow" Meow Mix theme song, and started a sensation. Fortunately, the cat managed to spit out the offending food and went on to live a long and happy life.

HOWARD HUGHES'S CAT

THE FELINE WHO HAD EVERY-
THING EXCEPT AN OWNER

Billionaire movie producer, aviation pioneer, and casino owner Howard Hughes was as incredibly famous as he was incredibly odd. The stories about his strangeness—from his dinnertime practice of sorting all his peas by size (he carried around a tiny rake for the purpose) to his obsession with designing the perfect brassiere for his amply endowed film protégée, Jane Russell—are legion. So it's probably no surprise that he reacted bizarrely when his wife, Jean Peters, told him that a rather dicey-looking tomcat she'd adopted had gone missing.

The name of the cat is lost to history, but Hughes's reaction to his departure is enshrined in the lexicon of eccentric anecdotes. According to the story, the billionaire launched a massive effort to locate the missing pet. He micromanaged the project from his mansion, demanding progress reports from his minions every hour on the hour. But when the poor cat was finally located hiding in an old barn, Hughes examined him personally and pronounced him unfit for his household.

This ignited a closely managed effort to find the

cat a suitable new residence. Several potential adoptive owners were interviewed extensively, then rejected for various reasons. After much debate, the feline was bundled off to a high-class cattery—the sort of cattery that seemed more than ready to cater to Hughes's oddball ideas of propriety. The tomcat took up residence in its own carpeted, tastefully decorated room, complete with a TV should it desire to catch a program.

The cattery required that former owners dash off a letter to their pets once each month. Hughes, eager to be rid of the problem, is said to have fobbed off the task on an underling. The writer was apparently still on the job—and the cat, presumably, was still enjoying his television-equipped suite—when Hughes passed away on April 5, 1976. Jean Peters, who had instigated the entire situation by taking in the feline in the first place, had divorced the erratic billionaire five years earlier.

PHET AND PLOY

THE CATS WHO GOT MARRIED

Every bride gets a bit testy as her big day approaches. But in the case of one Thai couple, the bride and groom were both quite catty. That's because they were Siamese cats named Phet and Ploy. Their 1996 Bangkok nuptials are considered the most opulent feline "wedding" on record.

Why do cats need to get married? According to their owner, cosmetics magnate Vicharn Charas-archa, it was only fair. Both felines were rare "diamond-eyed" cats, which according to Thai beliefs are extraordinarily lucky. Charas-archa became a believer after discovering the cats on the Thai/Burmese border and taking them in. Shortly thereafter, his struggling business started taking off.

So he shared the wealth by staging a wedding for his good luck charms at a Bangkok disco. The groom arrived by helicopter, and the bride (who came with a $40,000 dowry) by limousine. They wore a tuxedo and bridal gown and sported tiny wedding rings on their paws.

Post-wedding plans included a honeymoon river cruise and, sometime afterward, a trip to the vet. That's because the "diamond eyes" effect is caused by a form of glaucoma.

TIDDLES

THE FAT CAT CHAMPION
OF LONDON

The most beloved fictional character associated with London's venerable Paddington Station is undoubtedly Paddington Bear. There's even a gift shop at the cavernous train depot selling everything to do with its cuddly namesake. Of slightly more modest renown is the landmark's *other* animal mascot—Tiddles, the lavatory cat. His somewhat less heartwarming story began in 1970, when lavatory attendant June Watson adopted a six-week-old stray and started bringing him to work with her. Soon, as many people dropped by to visit the personable feline as to use the facilities.

They came bearing gifts of steak, chicken, lamb, and whatever other tidbits they thought would tempt the cat. The deluge of goodies became so overwhelming that Tiddles got his own personal fridge to store them. Not surprisingly, this lord of the ladies' loo soon swelled to royal girth. By 1982 he weighed so

much that he was named "London Fat Cat Champion."

Of course this was far from healthy, and visitors soon were discouraged from feeding him. But the goodies kept coming. Poor Tiddles, swollen to an ungainly thirty-two pounds, came to resemble a beach ball with fur. Though he eventually passed away from obesity-related health issues, it can safely be said that he died happy.

TONI

THE WORLD'S MOST ELIGIBLE FELINE BACHELOR

Is it possible to be too desirable? In the case of one hapless feline, it certainly was. Pity poor Toni, a cat with a pedigree so excruciatingly rare that he became an object of desire not only to aficionados, but to thieves.

His sorry tale began in June 2000, when British cat breeder Peter Collins heard someone snooping around the outdoor run used by Toni, his long-haired Turkish Angora. When Collins stepped outside, he saw a woman wearing orange glasses and a hooded jacket carrying his prized pet away in a basket. "I chased her and saw her getting into an estate car with foreign plates that had its engine running," he told the BBC. "She jumped in and the car roared off before I could reach it."

The heist, police surmised, was carefully planned and executed. But why would anyone go to so much trouble to nab a cat? Because Toni (full name Antonio B. Pinardin) was both exceedingly rare and exceedingly valuable (somewhere, experts guessed, in the neighborhood of £250,000). He'd been purchased a couple of years earlier by Collins and his wife, Joy, from a German breeder for the comparatively reasonable price of £1,500. But his stock soared after a catastrophe overtook his breed.

When he started life, Toni became one of a handful of absolutely pureblood long-haired Turkish Angoras in the world. He was born into a forty-year breeding program overseen by the Ankara Zoo and designed to save the felines, which were once favorites of European royalty, from extinction.

Toni's role as a stud cat was ordained before he was conceived. But then an outbreak of an AIDS-like virus at the Ankara Zoo devastated the breeding population, leaving Toni as the only male cat with top-notch bloodlines who was capable of reproducing. Not surprisingly, his value rose faster than an Internet stock before the dot-com bust. His stud fee alone was reckoned at around £600. Over his lifetime, this Secretariat of cats would fetch a fortune.

That cash is now most likely going into someone else's pockets. In spite of intervention by Interpol, no one has seen hide nor hair of Toni since his abduction. Police theorize that perhaps a German "collector" absconded with the cat. Collins reported that the woman said something in German as she dashed away.

One needn't worry about the conditions of Toni's imprisonment, however. Wherever he is, he's probably being treated well—and having lots and lots of intimate encounters with female cats. One hopes his new owner keeps a close eye on him and keeps his outdoor run securely locked.

DOCKET

THE LOST CAT WHO BECAME
A COLLECTOR'S ITEM

It's hard to tell where the private life of renowned London conceptual artist Tracey Emin ends and her very public professional life begins. She's worked in media ranging from paint to photography to appliquéd quilts. Her most famous piece was called, simply, *My Bed*. True to the name, it was her own unmade bed, surrounded by dirty clothes and other refuse. It caused an uproar in the art world, turning Emin into a celebrity. Today the piece is valued in the neighborhood of £150,000.

Clearly, almost anyone or anything can become part of her work—a fact that came back to bite her when her cat, Docket, ran away from home in 2002. Distraught, Emin posted handmade "lost kitty" posters around her neighborhood. Almost immediately they were taken down by collectors, who sold them for as much as £500. Flabbergasted, Emin put out the word that there was nothing in the least artistic about the hastily written notices. Fortunately, everything worked out in the end. The collectors got to keep their trophies, and Docket found his way home on his own.

FRANK

THE CAT WHO BECAME THE FIRST FELINE INTERNET PHENOMENON

Many artists suffer for their work, but few suffered as much as Internet celebrity Frank the Cat. In 2003, the search engine Yahoo! declared his Web offering to be one of its top sites of the year. All Frank did to gain such plaudits was lie quietly in a cage. Oh, and almost get himself killed.

The unlikely story began in January 2002, when Frank, an English cat residing in Cambridge, was hit by a car. The accident broke his pelvis, requiring reconstructive surgery and a lengthy recovery. The feline spent his convalescence piled up in a cage at the home of his master, David Donna, the managing partner of a small Internet firm.

Donna had an idea. Ostensibly to test some company software—but also, perhaps, because he thought it might be cool—he created a Web site chronicling Frank's ordeal, complete with pictures of his X-rays and a biography of his pet. As the *piece de resistance*, he rigged up two webcams so that surfers could watch every moment of Frank's recovery.

What took everyone by surprise was just how many people seemed interested in the injured cat's plight. Within minutes of going public, the site was getting two thousand hits per minute.

Unknown to Frank, who spent most of his time sleeping, close to five million people logged on to check up on him. But it couldn't last forever. Once the feline regained enough strength to get around on his own, he would no longer lie obligingly in front of the webcams for his fans.

Shortly after Frank's recovery, the live site was taken off the Web. In the aftermath, more than a few social commentators scratched their heads about what made it so popular. "It's just one of those things that has been blown out of all proportion," Donna told the BBC. The project did produce one unlooked-for benefit, however. A mysterious couple had assisted Frank shortly after his accident, probably saving his life. When they spotted him on the Internet, they got in touch with Donna, who arranged a meeting between the cat and his benefactors.

OTHER FELINES OF DISTINCTION

GRIMALKIN: The celebrated pet of French astrologer Nostradamus. Grimalkin was also the name of the witches' cat in Macbeth.

DELILAH: The favored pet of Freddie Mercury, front man for the famed British rock group Queen. The female tortoiseshell was immortalized in the song "Delilah," on the band's 1991 album Innuendo. The lyrics, while enumerating her good qualities, also take her to task for peeing in the house.

RUPI: The pet of Jethro Tull founder Ian Anderson and inspiration for the title song of his 2004 solo album Rupi's Dance.

JELLYLORUM: The feline owned by T. S. Elliot, who served as the inspiration for (and appears in) the book Old Possum's Book of Practical Cats. The collection of poems spawned the musical Cats.

KAROUN: Cat owned by famed French writer and film director Jean Cocteau. The distinctly feline makeup used for the Beast in his famous 1946 version of Beauty and the Beast was reportedly influenced by Karoun's features.

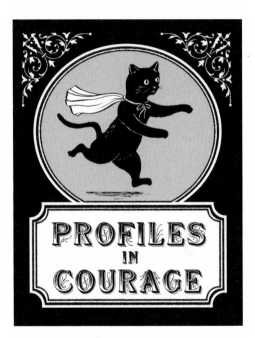

PROFILES IN COURAGE

SIMON
BRITAIN'S MOST-
DECORATED SEA CAT

Cats who live aboard ships need more than the usual amount of intestinal fortitude. They spend their lives surrounded by water, and if their ship happens to be a vessel of war, they may face combat as well.

Such was the case for Simon, who "served" aboard the British destroyer HMS *Amethyst*. He displayed such fortitude in the face of battle, loss, and injury that he became the first cat in English history to receive a medal for courage under fire.

He was born inauspiciously, on an island off the coast of Hong Kong. His sea service began in March 1948, when a sailor smuggled him aboard the *Amethyst*. He became a favorite of the captain, accompanying him on rounds and even sleeping in his cap. Simon was also an expert rat hunter, often laying out his kills at the feet of his commanding officer.

In 1949, the *Amethyst* received a new captain, who also appreciated Simon's company. The ship then got a new, more dangerous assignment. Mainland China was in the throes of the communist revolution, and the ship was to sail up the Yangtze River to Nanking to guard the British embassy and to evacuate the staff if Mao Zedong's forces took the town.

The *Amethyst* voyaged into a hornet's nest. Gun batteries on the banks of the Yangtze opened up on the ship, killing more than two dozen crewmen and inflicting heavy damage. While trying to evade the attacks, the ship ran aground on a sand bar. The captain's cabin took a direct hit, killing him and, everyone assumed, Simon as well. After a long struggle the crew finally refloated the ship and maneuvered out of range of shore fire. The wounded were evacuated and the dead buried.

About that time the crew realized that Simon had survived the destruction of the captain's cabin. But just barely. His whiskers were singed, he was covered with blood, and he was dehydrated and suffering from four shrapnel wounds. He was taken to sickbay and patched up, though his chances of survival seemed small.

But the indestructible cat had other ideas. Slowly he convalesced, eventually regaining enough strength to go rat hunting again. There was plenty of time for this, because the *Amethyst* was trapped behind enemy lines. Food was running short, and the ship's rodent population made desperate attempts to get at it. Simon, though hurt, was the first line of defense.

When not on rat patrol, the little cat was in sickbay, commiserating with convalescing sailors. His own injuries helped them relate to the cat and perhaps feel more at ease. He even managed to befriend the *Amethyst*'s new captain, who had made no secret of his dislike for felines. When he came down with a fever that confined him to his quarters, Simon dutifully sat on his bunk beside him.

Finally, after two months bottled up on the Yangtze, the *Amethyst* escaped under cover of darkness. The crew members were hailed as heroes, as was Simon. He was awarded the Dicken Medal for animal gallantry—the four-legged version of the Victoria Cross. So far he is the only cat ever to receive the honor.

Unfortunately, he never lived to see it. While sweating out a six-month mandatory quarantine after reaching England, he contracted an infection and died on November 28, 1949. Today, a stone marker stands over his grave. It says in part, and with typical British understatement, that the little cat's behavior "was of the highest order."

FAITH

THE CAT WHO DEFIED
THE LONDON BLITZ

The first days of World War II were dark ones indeed for Great Britain. Nazi Germany had conquered almost all of Europe, leaving the residents of the island nation to fight on alone. From September 1940 to May 1941, Hitler tried to crush England's will to resist by launching the Blitz—the indiscriminate terror bombing of cities, especially London.

Though thousands were killed and wounded, the nightly attacks failed to break the spirit of the people. Many, in the face of great danger, displayed unforgettable courage. And the heroism wasn't just confined to humans. One of the most famous stories concerns a church cat named Faith. In 1936, the little tabby found her way to St Augustine's and St Faith's Church in London. She took up residence in the rectory.

Faith attended all services in which the rector, Father Henry Ross (who had originally taken her in), took part. If her benefactor wasn't speaking, she sat in the front pew. If Ross was preaching, she sat in the pulpit at his feet.

In August 1940, Faith gave birth to a single male kitten, which the church choir celebrated the next Sunday by singing *All Things Bright and Beautiful*. The black and white puff ball was named Panda.

But on September 6 of that year, something strange happened. Faith, for no discernable reason, led Ross to the church basement and begged him to open the door. He complied, and later saw the mother cat carry Panda from his comfortable upstairs basket down to the dusty, dark sanctum. Three times Ross took the kitten back upstairs, and three times Faith carried him back down. Finally the pastor admitted defeat, took the kitten's basket to the basement, and tried to make the two as comfortable as possible.

Within days, however, Faith's odd behavior would seem more like clairvoyance.

On September 9, while Ross was away, his church took a direct hit from a bomb. He arrived to find emergency crews scrambling around the still-burning structure. Ross told them that to his knowledge the only creatures inside were Faith and Panda. The fireman he spoke to said there was no chance they could have survived.

But Ross couldn't accept that. Risking his life, he entered the building's sagging, flaming remains and called out for Faith. He heard a faint answering meow and dug through the rubble until he found the two felines buried under a pile of singed sheet music. Faith, grimy but uninjured, was sitting with her kitten beneath her, in the same place she'd scouted out days earlier. Ross quickly carried both cats to safety, getting clear just as the roof collapsed.

The story of the church cat's selfless devotion to her kitten soon spread across the United Kingdom. On October 12, 1945, before a packed house at the rebuilt St Augustine's and while nestled in the arms of the Archbishop of Canterbury, she received a special medal for her courage.

Panda, once grown, became the mascot of a retirement home. And Faith remained at the church until her death on September 28, 1948. Her passing was worldwide news, as was her burial near the churchyard gate. The feline described as "the bravest cat in the world" can spend eternity at the place she loved.

MRS. CHIPPY

THE CAT WHO EXPLORED
THE ANTARCTIC

Few adventure stories are as gripping as that of the Imperial Trans-Arctic Expedition of 1914–1916, led by famed explorer Ernest Shackleton. The expedition's original plan was to take the ship *Endurance* to the coast of Antarctica, then dispatch a team to sled from one end of the continent to the other. But a series of disasters turned the voyage of discovery into a battle for survival. In the end, it would claim the life of a much-loved crewmember—the *Endurance*'s cat, Mrs. Chippy.

The feline came aboard with the ship's carpenter, Henry McNeish. The crew called the cat Mrs. Chippy (*chippy* being slang for *carpenter*), and kept the *Mrs.* even after they realized the cat was a male. But whatever his sex, the feline earned his keep by killing the mice and rats that threatened the expedition's food stores.

When he wasn't hunting vermin or chumming around with the crew, Mrs. Chippy seemed intent on finding new ways to risk his life. The ship's deck was lined with sled dog kennels, which the cat loved to walk nonchalantly across. And one night, as the ship traversed the icy South Atlantic, the feline jumped out a porthole and into the inky sea. By some miracle he was spotted, and the ship turned in time to pick him up. He spent roughly ten minutes bobbing in the water—more than enough to kill an average human.

But his luck didn't hold. In January 1915, the *Endurance* got stuck in the ice far from the Antarctic coast. Months passed, but the grip of the elements never slackened. Finally, stores began to run low, and the weight of the floes started crushing the ship's hull, forcing the crew to live in tents out on the ice sheet. Shackleton decided to risk everything by abandoning ship and taking the entire crew, along with whatever gear and provisions they could carry or drag, 350 miles by open boat and sled to the nearest land. Everyone would go. Everyone except Mrs. Chippy. Shackleton decided that on such a desperate mission there was no place for a cat.

On the appointed day, the entire crew filed by to gaze their last upon the luckless feline, who had shared all their travails without complaint. After everyone said their goodbyes, the ship's steward served him his favorite meal—a bowl of sardines. And then, according to most accounts, Mrs. Chippy was dispatched, as humanely as possible, to that great scratching post in the sky. The *Endurance* crew abandoned ship shortly thereafter. They spent the next few months traversing the bitterly cold ocean in open boats and trudging across windswept tundra. But in the end, the entire (human) crew made it back to civilization alive.

Shackleton's leadership made him a hero. But he was no hero to Mrs. Chippy's owner, Henry McNeish. Apparently the ship's carpenter bore a grudge against his commanding officer for the rest of his life. After the expedition, he settled in New Zealand, where he lived until his death in 1930. Any mention of the polar expedition would inevitably bring up a bitter complaint about how Shackleton killed his cat.

The old carpenter did receive some solace, and come company, in the afterlife. In 2004 an addition was made to his Wellington grave. The slab that marks his final resting place was adorned with a life-sized bronze sculpture of his beloved companion, Mrs. Chippy.

FELIX

THE FIRST CAT IN SPACE

At the dawn of the space race, numerous non-human species, from chimps to dogs, were bundled aboard experimental rockets and fired into orbit. But while many remember Laika the dog and Ham the chimp, few now recall the otherworldly exploits of Felix, the first feline in space.

The former Paris street cat (there's some controversy as to whether it was a male or female) was scrupulously trained for his trip. On October 18, 1963, he was strapped into a Veronique AG1 sounding rocket at a French base in Algeria and blasted into the great beyond.

Felix didn't go into orbit, but he did fly more than 130 miles into space. Then the capsule reentered the atmosphere, deployed a parachute, and returned to terra firma. No one is sure what happened to Felix afterward, but one thing is certain: He fared better than the second cat in space, whose rocket

broke up in flight on October 24 of the same year.

Felix's journey is a bright spot in the history of catkind—tarnished only by the fact that the French put the first *rat* into space two years earlier.

THE CLIMBING KITTEN

THE CAT WHO CONQUERED
THE MATTERHORN

Few mountains boast as fearsome a reputation as the Matterhorn. Straddling the Swiss/Italian border, its forbidding slopes defied mountaineers until the middle of the nineteenth century, when it was finally scaled. Yet even today, the 14,693-foot peak still claims several unwary climbers each year. Clearly, this challenge is not for the young and inexperienced.

Unless you happen to be a cat.

The first feline ascent of this famous Alpine peak was accomplished in August 1950 during an expedition led by Edmund Biner. While guiding his group up the Matterhorn, he paused at 12,556 feet to get his bearings. It was then that the adventurers realized they were being followed—by a kitten. A four-month-old kitten belonging to one Josephine Aufdenblatten of Geneva.

History doesn't explain why the kitten elected to follow the men—only that it eventually pursued them all the way to the summit. Figuring the beleaguered creature had used up more than a couple of its nine lives, one of the climbers carried it back down to sea level in his rucksack.

SCARLETT

THE CAT WHO BECAME
AN ACTION HERO

Overnight, a scrawny New York City feline went from anonymous stray to international hero. The transformation happened, literally, in a flash.

A flash of fire, that is. The saga began in March 1996, when a blaze consumed an East New York garage. As the battle against the conflagration wound down, firefighters noticed three four-week-old kittens huddled near the building's front door, crying in fear. Across the street sat two more. A badly burned calico female paced nervously between the two groups.

It didn't take long for firefighter David Giannelli to figure out what had happened. Giannelli, whose soft spot for pets earned him the nickname "the animal guy" in East New York's Ladder Company 75, guessed that during the fire, the mother cat had dashed repeatedly into the blaze to rescue her kittens. Now she was in the process, in spite of her severe injuries, of moving them to a new hiding place.

The firefighter scooped up the mother and babies and took them to the North Shore Animal League in Port Washington, New York. The staff, sensing a chance for a little publicity, told the story to a local TV station. The agency got more than a *little* publicity. Everyone from CNN to the BBC picked up the tale, and soon people from as far away as Cairo and Japan were writing and phoning the shelter.

The mother was named Scarlett, because of the livid color of her burns. Sadly, one of the kittens died of an infection. But the other four made strong recoveries. As the family convalesced together, thousands of adoption offers flooded in from around the world. Finally, two kittens named Samsara and Tanuki were given to a Port Washington family; the other two, Cinders and Oreo, found their way to Hampton Bays, New York.

Heroic Scarlett found a home with the Wellen family in Brooklyn. Her scars healed, and the only remaining signs of her travails were her rather poor vision and the amputated tips of her ears. Her new owners have also helped heal any emotional scars. "She's a total love machine," a family member told the *New York Times*. The formerly scrawny stray is also, apparently, an eating machine. After her rescue she ballooned to seventeen pounds—quite a change from her days as an action heroine.

MOURKA

THE CAT WHO SERVED AT STALINGRAD

No single World War II battle proved as costly as the struggle for Stalingrad. For 199 days, German forces tried to wrest control of the Soviet city (now called Volgograd) from the Red Army. The Nazis were finally repelled, but at the almost unimaginable cost of two million lives.

The victory demanded incredible feats of heroism. Remarkably, one of the bravest of the brave wasn't a soldier, but a cat named Mourka. During the bitter street fighting inside the city, exposing oneself for even a moment was tantamount to suicide. For one squad assigned to find and report the location of German artillery positions, the only way to get information back to headquarters was by hand—until they received unexpected help in the form of Mourka. The stray cat could run notes back and forth unobserved, sparing his human comrades terrible risk. His contribution to the war effort was duly noted in the *Times* (UK), which said of the intrepid feline: "He has shown himself worthy of Stalingrad, and whether for cat or man there can be no higher praise."

PRECIOUS

THE CAT WHO SURVIVED 9/11

During a crisis, average citizens may discover they possess undreamed-of reserves of heroism and grit. Such was the case for many New Yorkers on September 11, 2001. And such was especially the case for a pampered nine-pound Persian cat named Precious. Her tale of survival is as unlikely as it is inspiring.

Precious's owners, Steve and D. J. Kerr, were out of town on the fateful day. The cat was alone in their apartment, located directly across the street from the Twin Towers, when the buildings collapsed. The shock shattered every window, first spraying the interior with glass and metal shrapnel and then filling it with a cloud of dust.

But things got worse. The 114 Liberty Street building was so heavily damaged that its tenants weren't allowed to return. That meant Precious had to survive on her own—a tall order for an eight-year-old feline who'd never even been outside. Yet eighteen days later, an animal rescue team found her on the building's roof. She was thirsty, dirty, and two pounds lighter, but otherwise intact. Her survival proved that New Yorkers are tough, even the ones who don't get out much.

TOMMY

THE CAT WHO COULD
USE A PHONE

The news is filled with stories of dogs who help their stricken owners. But few canines have ever displayed the devotion, let alone the cognitive skills, shown by Tommy, owned by Gary Rosheisen of Columbus, Ohio. In January 2006, the chronically ill Rosheisen fell out of his wheelchair near his bed. He couldn't get up, and he couldn't call for help.

Shortly thereafter, someone used his phone to place a 911 call. When dispatchers answered, all they heard was silence on the other end. The call was disconnected and the number dialed, and when no one answered, police were dispatched. The officers who entered the apartment found an incapacitated Rosheisen sprawled on the bedroom floor and his orange and tan feline, Tommy, sitting in the living room by the phone. No one else was around. Later, Rosheisen (who must have had a lot of time on his hands) stated that he'd tried to teach his cat to hit the 911 button on his speed dial. He didn't think the lesson had stuck, but apparently it had. "He's my hero," he told the Associated Press.

EMILY

THE CAT WHO TRAVELED
WORST-CLASS TO FRANCE

Curiosity doesn't always kill the cat. More often, it just lands the cat in some very curious predicaments. That's certainly the case for Emily, a nondescript tabby who lived the first months of her life with owner Lesley McElhiney of Appleton, Wisconsin.

Emily had a nose for trouble. One day, while out roaming the neighborhood, she decided to explore a nearby warehouse. That decision started her on an adventure that spanned two continents and turned her into an international celebrity.

Because Emily can't talk, we'll never know all the details of her globetrotting adventure. But the high points of her itinerary are plain enough. In late September 2005, Emily started poking around a paper company distribution center near her home. Somehow she got into a container of paper bales bound for France. Once inside, she must have fallen asleep—so soundly, apparently, that she didn't notice when the container was sealed and shipped out.

She wouldn't see the light of day again for weeks. First the parcel containing the paper (and Emily) was hauled by truck to Chicago, then by ship to Belgium, then by truck again to Raflatac, a laminating company based in Nancy, France. Finally, on October 24 (which happened to be the hapless cat's first birthday), the crate was pried open to reveal a very thin, very thirsty Emily. Surprised workers checked her tags and called her Wisconsin veterinarian, who in turn informed the extremely surprised McElhiney family.

The tale of the little cat's saga quickly spread around the world, and volunteers stepped forward to help the far-ranging feline find her way home. Raflatac covered the $7-per-day cost of her mandatory month-long quarantine in France. And when Emily was finally cleared to return, she did so courtesy of Continental Airlines, which flew her back to the United States in business class. She'd grown so enamored of French food that she arrived home a bit plumper than when she left.

Emily was reunited with her family at the Milwaukee airport, and she resumed the life of quiet anonymity she'd lived before her fateful encounter with the shipping crate. "She seems a little calmer than she was before," McElhiney told the BBC. "Just a little quieter, a little, maybe, wiser."

RUSIK

THE CAT WITH A NOSE FOR (STOLEN) CAVIAR

Police dogs are old news. Police cats, however, are something special. Especially when they give their lives on the job. Such is the story of a Russian feline named Rusik.

Rusik's nose made him special. He had been adopted by customs guards at a police checkpoint in Stavropol, on the shores of the Caspian Sea. The guards soon learned he could infallibly detect the presence of caviar. This skill would have been useless almost anywhere except near the Caspian, whose sturgeon produce 95 percent of the world's high-quality caviar. Not surprisingly, numerous poachers net Caspian fish illegally, steal their roe, then smuggle it out for sale on the black market.

Enter Rusik, who was so good at locating concealed caviar in vehicles that he replaced the sniffer dog the cops formerly used. Alas, his career ended tragically in July 2003. After inspecting a bus, he jumped out onto the street and was run over by a car—a car in which he'd previously found contraband fish eggs. Was it a contract killing? Many suspect so. Especially since another police cat died a short while afterward, allegedley from eating a poisoned mouse.

SPARKY

THE CAT WHO SURVIVED
11,000 VOLTS

Cats supposedly have nine lives, but sometimes they don't use them wisely. Such was the case for one overly curious British tomcat. The feline made national headlines in March 1998, when he wandered into an electrical substation near his home in the town of Hull. There he somehow managed to short out the equipment, taking an 11,000-volt blast in the process, which is normally enough juice to kill a cat, a human being, or a herd of elephants, for that matter.

Yet somehow the cat survived. A Yorkshire Electricity employee spotted him shortly after the accident, extricated the limp, smoking feline from the equipment, and got him medical attention. His miraculous survival earned him television and newspaper coverage across Great Britain, along with a new nickname: Sparky.

Sparky did not get away from the encounter scot-free, however. His fur and paws were severely burned, his front leg injured, his ears paralyzed, and his whiskers incinerated. But his new look wasn't enough to prevent his horrified owners, Steve Bateman and Tricia Watts, from recognizing his picture in the paper. Explaining that his real name was Soxy, they stepped forward to claim their newfound celebrity.

The public, however, refused to relinquish its grip. Soxy/Sparky became a regular at public events and a popular mascot for charitable causes. He even won a national cat of the year award. "He was very loyal and affectionate, and he loved all the attention he got," Bateman told the BBC.

The only thing he lacked was the ability to learn from his mistakes. Despite the fact that his poor judgment and survival skills had been amply demonstrated, Bateman and Watts continued to let their pet roam the neighborhood. Finally, in September 1999, Sparky didn't return home. Suspecting the worst, his owners asked the folks at the electrical substation to poke around the equipment. Sure enough, they found Sparky. But this time his luck had run out.

In a heartbeat, the cat who had been a symbol of survival became a symbol of something far more important: The need to keep one's pets indoors. The cat who couldn't leave well enough alone will never roam again. He's confined for eternity to a small grave in his owners' garden.

TRIXY

THE CAT WHO BROKE INTO
THE TOWER OF LONDON

Cats have many fascinating and endearing qualities. However, steadfast, unyielding loyalty usually isn't one of them. That's what makes the story of Trixy, the favorite pet of Henry Wriothesley, third Earl of Southampton (1573–1624), so amazing. If her story can be believed, she displayed a level of devotion few *humans* can aspire to, let alone felines.

In his day, her master, the earl, was a well-known adventurer and patron of the arts. Shakespeare received both his encouragement and his funds. Unfortunately, the man also had a notoriously short temper and a penchant for backing the wrong horse during political disputes. His most disastrous miscalculation was joining with the Earl of Essex in a plot to overthrow Queen Elizabeth I. For this he earned a death sentence, which was shortly converted to life imprisonment in the Tower of London.

The earl began his sentence in 1601. While he cooled his heels in a tiny cell, his black and white cat, Trixy, grew agitated by his continued absence from Southampton House, the family seat. One day she simply walked away from the palatial estate, made her way via alleys and rooftops to the heart of London, located her master's cell, and entered it via a chimney. She spent the next two years at the earl's side, until Elizabeth's death and the ascension of James I led to Wriothesley and Trixy's release.

It seems nearly impossible that a pampered country cat could have made it all the way to the Tower on foot. How, exactly, did she know her master was there? Some surmise that she got some help from her human friends. Perhaps, it is said, the earl's wife smuggled Trixy into the prison.

No one, at this late date, will ever know the exact circumstances. But one thing is certain. The earl was greatly impressed by his little cat's fortitude and fidelity. Shortly after his release from the Tower, he commissioned a portrait of himself by painter John de Critz. It features Wriothesley garbed in the full finery of an English noble, standing alongside Trixy, who wears an appropriately steadfast scowl—just the sort of look one would expect from so intrepid a cat.

TRIM
THE FIRST CAT TO CIRCUMNAVIGATE AUSTRALIA

Landlubbers think dogs are man's best friend. But sailors pay their highest respect to cats. Their uncanny balance serves them well on pitching decks, and their hunting prowess keeps the rodents out of the biscuits. But even given this innate mutual respect, the relationship between famed explorer Matthew Flinders and his cat, Trim, was exceptional.

The two met in 1797 on the high seas. Both served aboard the HMS *Reliance*. One day Trim, who was still a kitten, was washed overboard—yet he somehow managed to swim back to the ship, snag a rope with his claws, and use it to climb aboard. Flinders, impressed, made him his own.

From 1801 to 1803, Flinders, now in command of the *Investigator*, slowly circumnavigated Australia, becoming the first person to do so. Trim, who never left his side, became the first *feline* to do so. But when the mission ended and the duo tried to get back to England, their return ship, the *Porpoise*, ran aground on the Great Barrier Reef. Incredibly, Flinders (with Trim at his side) navigated one of the wrecked ship's boats some 700 miles over open sea to Sydney, where he arranged for the rescue of the rest of the crew.

Flinders tried again to reach England on the schooner *Cumberland*. But he put in at the French-controlled island of Mauritius, not knowing that England and France were at war. He was thrown in a local prison for seven years. It was there that he and Trim finally parted. The cat kept him company for a while, until one day he simply disappeared—captured and eaten, Flinders guessed, by some of the island's underfed slave population.

When Flinders finally returned to England, he authored a book called *A Voyage to Terra Australis*, which popularized the use of the word *Australia*. Today his name can be found on natural landmarks and public buildings all over that continent, including a statue at Sydney's Mitchell Library. Behind it, perched on a window ledge, sits a bronze statue of Trim. It includes a tribute from his grieving master, who called him "the best and most illustrious of his race, the most affectionate of friends, faithful of servants, and best of creatures."

GRANPA

THE WORLD'S OLDEST CAT

These days, pampered felines enjoy the best food, accommodations, and medical care money can buy. So it isn't unusual to hear of well-preserved pets who live for twenty years or more. But few—actually, none—can match the record for longevity achieved by Granpa, who lived to the slightly overripe age of thirty-four years, two months, and four hours—good enough to earn him a spot in the *Guinness Book of World Records*.

Granpa's life was as strange as it was long. A rare hairless sphinx, he was taken to the Humane Society of Travis County (Texas) on January 16, 1970, by a good Samaritan who found him running loose near a busy intersection. He was almost immediately adopted by Jake Perry, a plumber, part-time cat show enthusiast, and feline rescuer. Figuring such an unusual cat must have a worried owner somewhere, he put up posters about him around town. Months later he received a call from a Frenchwoman, who in December 1969 had come to the United States to visit her daughter. While there her cat, Pierre, had escaped through an unlatched screen door, never to be seen again.

By that time Perry had owned the male sphinx, whom he had renamed Granpa Rexs Allen, for quite a while. Nevertheless, he agreed to let the woman have a look at him. After confirming that it was indeed her cat, she graciously allowed his benefactor to keep him. She even handed over his pedigree papers, which stated that he was born early on the morning of February 1, 1964, in Paris.

A few years later, Perry started entering Granpa in shows sponsored by the International Cat Association under the "household pet" category. To his great surprise, the feline, who was already into his second decade and thus considered old, earned the rank of supreme grand master, the highest possible award for pets in his division.

As his age reached the high twenties, Granpa's fame grew. Each year for his birthday, he got a vanilla cake topped with tuna and broccoli icing. Not surprisingly, he was generally the only one to partake. The rest of his unusual diet, however, would have passed muster with most human diners: Breakfast consisted of Egg Beaters, chopped bacon, broccoli or asparagus, and coffee. He also enjoyed either jelly or mayonnaise smeared on his food; he would choose which one every morning by putting his paw on the jar he preferred.

Fortified by lots of vegetables, Granpa persisted into his early thirties, which is roughly 150 in cat years. Finally, on April 1, 1998, he gave up the ghost after a long bout with pneumonia. After an elaborate funeral, during which Perry's numerous other cats viewed Granpa as he lay in state inside a tiny, lace-lined coffin, he was interred in his owner's backyard pet cemetery, which already contained about two dozen cats. Roughly four hundred fans from around the world sent cards, flowers, and other mementos.

His final honor was, of necessity, posthumous. The 2000 edition of the *Guinness Book of World Records* duly recognized the wizened French expatriate as the oldest cat who ever lived. His record just barely squeezes out the previous record holder, an English cat named Ma who survived for thirty-four years and one day. It just goes to show that in longevity, as in any other endeavor, persistence is key.

OTHER FELINES OF DISTINCTION

HAMLET: A Canadian cat who escaped from his pet carrier during a flight from Toronto. Hamlet remained at large on the plane for seven weeks, during which he flew a staggering 370,000 miles, making him history's most-traveled feline.

ANDY: A pet of U.S. Senator Ken Myer, Andy survived a sixteen-story (roughly 200-foot) fall from an apartment balcony and survived.

CHOUX: During World War I, a French soldier wanted to tell a German soldier who was married to his cousin that he'd become a father. So he tied a note to a kitten named Choux, who marched blithely across no–man's land to deliver the birth announcement.

PATSY: Accompanied famed aviator Charles Lindbergh on many flights, but not on the solo jaunt across the Atlantic that made him famous. "It's too dangerous a journey to risk a cat's life," Lindbergh reportedly said.

DUSTY: A monument to motherhood, this Texas feline bore 420 kittens in her lifetime, making her the most prolific cat in recorded history. Her record has lasted more than half a century.